BOOK NO: 1865805

KU-504-766

This book is due for return on or before the last date shown below.

 David Fulton Publishers

David Fulton Publishers Ltd
The Chiswick Centre, 414 Chiswick High Road, London W4 5TF
www.fultonpublishers.co.uk

First published in Great Britain in 2004 by David Fulton Publishers

Note: The right of the author to be identified as the author of this work has been asserted by him in accordance with the Copyright, Designs and Patents Act 1988.

David Fulton Publishers is a division of Granada Learning Limited, part of ITV plc.

British Library Cataloguing in Publication Data
A catalogue record for this book is available from the British Library.

ISBN 1 84312 118 2

Typeset by Mark Heslington, Northallerton, North Yorkshire
Printed and bound in Great Britain

Other titles of interest:

Inclusive Education: Diverse Perspectives
Melanie Nind, Kieron Sheehy, Katy Simmons, Jonathan Rix (eds)

Inclusive Education: Learners and Learning Contexts
Melanie Nind, Kieron Sheehy, Katy Simmons (eds)

Support Services and Mainstream Schools
Mike Blamires and John Moore

Inclusive Pedagogy in the Early Years
Phyllis Jones

Contents

Acknowledgements   iv

The Author   v

Chapter 1   Introduction   1

Chapter 2   Defining SEN: Distinguishing Goal-directed Need and Unconditional Need   11

Chapter 3   School Equal Opportunity Policies: Equality and Discrimination   27

Chapter 4   Funding through School Clusters: Self-interest and Co-operativeness   41

Chapter 5   Parents, LEA and SENDIST: Balance of Power   51

Chapter 6   The Special Educational Needs Forum: Representation   63

Chapter 7   Educating Pupils with Profound and Multiple Learning Difficulties: Rationality and
             Autonomy   75

Chapter 8   Including Pupils with SEN: Rights and Duties   87

             Bibliography   101

             Index   105

Acknowledgements

Chapter 2: Diane Whalley (SEN Regional Partnership, North West) was very helpful in suggesting contacts in LEAs developing criteria. Peter Edmundson, Assistant Director Pupil Services, Blackpool Borough Council, provided generous assistance with the case study in this chapter.

Chapter 3: I am grateful to Lyn Hurst, head teacher, for assistance with this chapter.

Chapter 4: Bill Hitchcock (SEN Regional Partnership, Yorkshire and the Humber) was very helpful in suggesting contacts in LEAs and private companies working on funding through school clusters. Glenn Allgood, SEN Manager, Education Bradford, kindly provided information for the case study.

Chapter 5: A parent, who wishes to remain anonymous, kindly provided the case study.

Chapter 6: Nick Knapman (SEN Regional Partnership, South West) kindly suggested contacts in LEAs having SEN forums. Miles Hapgood, Directorate Manager, Children and Family services, Exeter Primary Care Trust, and Jeanette Lee, Parent Partnership Liaison Manager, Devon Parent Partnership Services, were very helpful in providing information for the case study.

Chapter 7: Rob Ashdown, head teacher, St Luke's School, Scunthorpe, kindly helped with the case study.

Chapter 8: Tony Lingard, Head of Learning Support, Cornwall, provided assistance with making contacts. Bill Gribble, formerly with Flintshire LEA, helpfully drew my attention to the model of behaviour support to which he had contributed.

General

I owe particular thanks to Gerald Ackroyd, former senior educational psychologist, London; Fintan Bradley, Area Inclusion Manager, Cheshire LEA; and the Reverend Susan Bull, Surrey, who read the whole text and made invaluable comments.

Linda Evans of David Fulton Publishers provided generous help and support throughout.

The Author

Having trained as a teacher and as a research psychologist (Institute of Psychiatry), Michael Farrell taught pupils ranging from very able to those with profound and multiple learning difficulties. He has worked as a head teacher, a lecturer at the London University Institute of Education and as an LEA inspector for special education. After managing a national psychological project at City University he directed a project for the then Department for Education and Employment, developing materials and course structures for teacher education. He is currently a special education consultant with local education authorities, schools, voluntary organisations, universities and others, both in Britain and abroad. Author of many articles on education and psychology, he has also edited educational books. Among his other publications are: *The Blackwell Handbook of Education* (with Kerry and Kerry) (Blackwell, 1995); *The Special Education Handbook* (3rd edn) (David Fulton, 2002); *Key Issues for Primary Schools* (Routledge, 2000); *Key Issues for Secondary Schools* (Routledge, 2001); *Standards and Special Educational Needs* (Continuum, 2001); *Understanding Special Educational Needs* (Routledge, 2003); *Special Educational Needs: A Resource for Practitioners* (Sage/Paul Chapman, 2004).

This book is dedicated to
my dear friends Jim and
Alison Hewitt

Introduction

Benjamin Disraeli, presented with an unwanted book by its author, thanked his benefactor and mischievously added, 'I shall lose no time in reading it'. In the hope that potential readers of this text will be more persuadable, I set out below what this chapter, as a means of entry to the book as a whole, seeks to do, namely:

- identify proposed readers;
- outline the book's purpose;
- explain the book's structure.

Readers

This book is intended particularly for:

- SEN co-ordinators and all staff working with them;
- specialist SEN teachers;
- head teachers and aspirant head teachers on training courses;
- special school staff;
- LEA officers, including educational psychologists;
- officers and others working for the social services and the health service;
- those working for voluntary bodies involved with children and young people having SEN.

The purpose of the book

The book seeks to illustrate how aspects of special education can be better understood when seen in the context of certain concepts (ideas and values) that partly underpin those aspects. For example, I suggest, in Chapter 5, that an important influence in the relationship between parents, the LEA and the SENDIST is the powers of each and how they interact. A consideration of the notion of power, highlighting different types, is therefore a useful way of understanding this relationship.

The chapter titles of the book listed below, and their respective subtitles, indicate the aspect of SEN to be considered (e.g. the special educational needs forum) and the underpinning concept(s) (e.g. representation).

- Defining SEN: goal-directed need and unconditional need
- School equal opportunity policies: equality and discrimination
- Funding through school clusters: self-interest and co-operativeness
- Parents, the local education authority and the Special Educational Needs and Disability Tribunal: balance of power
- The Special Educational Needs Forum: representation
- Educating pupils with profound and multiple learning difficulties: rationality and autonomy
- Including pupils with SEN: rights and duties

Structure of the book

Each chapter has its own introduction, headlined sections, a case study and a summary/conclusion. At the end of the book there is a bibliography and an index.

Chapter 2: Defining SEN: goal-directed need and unconditional need

This chapter considers the importance, to the local education authority, schools, parents and others of agreeing how SEN will be defined. It relates this to the issue of distinguishing between goal-directed needs (of which there may be a justification in satisfying) and unconditional needs (of which there may be no justification in satisfying).

The chapter first looks at former categories of handicap used in England and at some criticisms of categories. It then examines the current legal definition of SEN in England and the notions of goal-directed need and unconditional need before focusing on the interpretation of each in relation to SEN.

I review the circumstances in which unconditional need may be regarded as goal-related need. Such a confusion can, I suggest, contribute to the unjustified expansion of 'needs' that the education system is expected to meet. I emphasise the importance of defining SEN as one way of trying to avoid an unjustified increase in the number of pupils with supposed 'needs'. The related matters of 'areas of need' and the continuing and increasing use of categories are considered as ongoing attempts to refine definitions of SEN.

A case study illustrates the efforts of an LEA in developing definitions of SEN to help in identifying and assessing pupils with SEN.

Chapter 3: School equal opportunity policies: equality and discrimination

Written school policies may be based on a view of equal opportunities that makes assumptions taking insufficient account of dilemmas regarding equality and discrimination. This chapter looks at difficulties surrounding the concept of equality and whether there can be negative implications of seeking equality. This leads to a consideration of the contested nature of the concept of equality of opportunity.

I explore problems of relating discrimination to ideas of not allowing people's lives to be affected by circumstances not under their control. A further definition of discrimination is examined which relates to treating people with undeserved contempt, but this is also considered to have drawbacks. A position is considered which suggests that one should seek for others to be in a good enough position – not necessarily being equal – although further difficulties arise in determining what is good enough.

In the light of this, the definition of discrimination in the Special Educational Needs and Disability Act 2001 (SENDA) is reviewed. The implications of the issues discussed in this chapter for school policies for pupils with SEN and equal opportunities are examined. I suggest that underlying such policies is not the principle of equality and the avoidance of discrimination but the principle of treating children unequally (that is treating pupils with SEN preferentially) and discriminating in favour of them. This is justified because of the difficulties and disabilities that pupils with SEN experience. This relates to the issue that, educationally, pupils with SEN are likely to require preferential treatment to move nearer to a position in which they can more readily benefit from the opportunities of which other children can more easily take advantage. Confusion can arise if this approach to pupils with SEN is combined in a policy taking a different approach to equality and discrimination for other pupils; for example, those from different ethnic minority groups or from different social backgrounds.

A case study presents a school's policies relating to equal opportunities with particular reference to sections on SEN.

Chapter 4: Funding through school clusters: self-interest and co-operativeness

The development of approaches to SEN funding using school clusters involves balancing various responsibilities and interests of schools, the LEA, parents and others.

One way of interpreting this is in terms of the degree of self-interest or co-operativeness required or demonstrated by the parties involved.

Self-interest could explain parents, schools, lobby groups and others maximising resources for their own children who are considered to have SEN, in a redistributive society, without necessarily having regard to the fair and equitable distribution of resources for others, including other children with SEN. A view that co-operativeness overrides self-interest could justify approaches such as the distribution of money to schools through school clusters.

However, such an approach could equally be interpreted as assuming essential self-interest and circumventing or harnessing it. In the light of this, a case study examines LEA funding and school clusters.

Whatever view is taken of 'self-interest' and 'co-operativeness', each is likely to come to the fore in different circumstances and at different times. This makes it important that a system of checks and balances is maintained that can help ensure fair and equitable funding.

Chapter 5: Parent, LEA and SENDIST: balance of power

In this chapter I consider the relationship between politics, power and resources. I explain the nature of decision-making power and then consider the notion in relation to SEN focusing on the power to identify pupils at Early Years Action/School Action; Early Years Action Plus/School Action Plus; and in relation to statutory assessment.

Mention is made of guidance on preventing and resolving disagreements between parents and local education authorities concerning SEN. Turning to a consideration of the Special Educational Needs and Disability Tribunal (SENDIST), the chapter outlines the role of the Tribunal. It then looks at the appeals to the SENDIST in terms of the power of parent lobby groups and of tensions between LEA powers and those of the SENDIST.

In a case study, the parent of a child with autism gives her account of the process of getting a statement for her child and of appealing to the SEN Tribunal.

Chapter 6: The Special Educational Needs Forum: representation

Among the fora in education are regional and local ones that focus on SEN issues, perhaps bringing together parents, officers for the education, health and social services and others. Any SEN forum that seeks to hear and discuss differing views assumes that participants represent, in some way, others who cannot be present. In this chapter, there-fore, representation is defined and some criticisms of representation in a capitalist liberal democracy are outlined. Different forms of representation are considered: choosing people with a good education and with wide experience, mandated represen-tation and characteristic representation.

I examine the influence of children's views and child advocacy, disability interest groups and parent groups in special education. The chapter considers the *Special Educational Needs Code of Practice* (Department for Education and Skills 2001b) guidance which seeks to include, in the identification of SEN and subsequent provision, the views of children either directly or through advocacy. I look at the particular role of disability groups as lobbyists. The chapter examines whether an unrelated person with, say, a physical disability can represent a child, for example, with profound and multiple learning difficulties simply because both can be, apparently, brought together under a broad conception of disability. Such narrow notions of representation are considered as a recipe for social division and conflict. The role of parents is considered, including the extent to which parents can represent children with SEN.

A case study is presented describing the formation and operation of an 'SEN forum' for the parents and carers of children with SEN which has developed links with officers from the education, social and health services and others. It is suggested that if potential and real difficulties and issues are addressed, attempts to develop consensus through dialogue by such means as SEN fora can be worthwhile, despite the problematic nature of representation.

Chapter 7: Educating pupils with profound and multiple learning difficulties: rationality and autonomy

This chapter considers 'reason' and 'free will' in terms of liberal theory. It suggests that liberal thought is weak in offering protection against discrimination for people with PMLD to the extent that they are considered to lack the powers of reason and free will that constitute the notion of a moral person in liberal theory. Against this background I consider the moral convictions and motives of parents who care for children with PMLD.

Those who educate children with PMLD, it is suggested, may be motivated by moral values similar to those of parents of children with PMLD and by other convictions. Teachers and others involved in the education of these children may not use considerations of rationality and free will to justify their commitment. However, these educators still value the powers of rationality and free will as expressed in their attempts to encourage these in pupils as reflected in curricula and approaches to teaching and learning considered suitable for pupils with PMLD.

A case study illustrates how, in teaching pupils with PMLD, teachers and schools assume that pupils can be initiated into an approach to the curriculum that encourages rationality and autonomy.

Chapter 8: Including pupils with SEN: rights and duties

As this chapter concerns the 'rights' associated with inclusion, I first explain the particular aspect of inclusion under consideration. I examine what inclusion is (or, more accurately, what I am focusing on for the purpose of this chapter). In specifying what aspect of inclusion is being discussed I explain who I am referring to and where the inclusion would take place. The chapter then looks at why inclusion might be justified and how and when it might take place.

The chapter concentrates on legal rights, outlining four types. I then consider examples of rights in special education: the right to be educated in the mainstream and the civil rights of disabled pupils relating to inclusion. The duties of the local education authority and others are considered to clarify the nature of the 'inclusion right'. The rights of others that compete with the 'inclusion right' are examined. Both the duties of the LEA and the rights of others indicate the boundaries on the 'right' to inclusion. A case study sets out an LEA behaviour support model.

Special education and inclusion

Including everyone

One of the themes of inclusion is a tendency to think in terms of including everyone, although it is not always specified what to include them in. For example, such a broad view may be seen in the training booklet connected with Ofsted courses on the inspection of school inclusion (Office for Standards in Education 2000: 1). This states that educational inclusion is 'more than a concern with one group of pupils such as those who have been or are likely to be excluded from school'. Rather, it is about equal opportunities for all pupils 'whatever their age, gender, ethnicity, attainment or background'. The 'different groups' of pupils concerned include:

- girls and boys;
- minority ethnic and faith groups, travellers, asylum seekers and refugees;
- pupils who need support to learn English as an additional language;
- pupils with special educational needs;
- gifted and talented pupils;
- children 'looked after' by the local authority;
- other children, such as sick children; young carers; those from families under stress; pregnant schoolgirls and teenage mothers; and
- any pupils who are at risk of disaffection and exclusion.

(Office for Standards in Education 2000: 1)

A concern with such a view of inclusion is that by making it so wide the particular requirements of pupils with SEN, as well as those of other particular groups, may be overlooked. It may be argued that children and young people are not defined merely by their SEN in isolation but also by other features such as their gender, ethnic group and social background. If this is taken into account, schools will be able to provide better for the whole child. However, it is also important that the particular knowledge and skills associated with providing for pupils with SEN do not get lost in an approach that seeks to be all-encompassing (see also Farrell 2003a: 27–9).

Avoiding negative aspects of labelling

Related to this concern about the all-embracing nature of inclusion is the assumption that labelling is, inevitably, largely negative. In the case of special education, one response to this supposed negative impact of labelling has been to periodically change the labels.

In the case of pupils now considered to have severe learning difficulties, previous terminology included:

- imbeciles (Mental Deficiency Act 1913);
- severely subnormal (Education Act 1944);
- educationally sub-normal (severe) (Education [Handicapped Children] Act 1970).

(Farrell 1998: 16)

Pupils that were once considered 'maladjusted' became pupils with 'emotional and behavioural difficulties' (EBD) and, more recently, pupils with 'behavioural, emotional and social difficulties' (BESD).

Such changes did not, of course, simply reflect a wish to change the label but were intended to signal that not everything that can be said about a pupil has been said when one uses, for example, the term 'maladjusted'. The different terminology at least allowed that here, first, was a pupil and, secondly, that among ways of regarding him is the judgement that he has EBD. Even this attempt to avoid equating the pupil with the label by referring to a pupil with a difficulty is not consistent as the current interchange-ability of terms such as 'pupil with dyslexia' and 'dyslexic pupil' or 'pupil with autism' and 'autistic pupil' indicates.

But set against this concern not to label negatively is the view that identification and assessment are essential for pupils with SEN. For example, if a pupil with SEN is not identified and assessed accurately and fairly (e.g. using criteria), then the resources and support that may be appropriate for the pupil may be diverted elsewhere. They may, for example, go to other pupils thought by some schools and some parents to have 'needs' but who do not, as legally defined (and increasingly as locally agreed), have SEN. This is indicated in Chapter 2, 'Defining SEN: distinguishing goal-directed need and uncon-ditional need'.

There is a further difficulty in not clearly identifying and assessing a pupil with SEN and considering the pupil together with other foci for inclusion such as 'minority ethnic and faith groups, travellers, asylum seekers and refugees' (Ofsted 2000: 1). This is that policies intended to benefit pupils with SEN can become too diffuse. An example is seen in Chapter 3, 'School equal opportunity policies: equality and discrimination'. In the light of that chapter, it will be seen that there is an argument for a separate policy for pupils with SEN to ensure unequal treatment and positive discrimination while policies for other pupils set out aims to assure equal treatment and to avoid discrimination.

Once identification is agreed and preferential provision is set out in policy it is important that preferential funding is directed where it is required. Ways of balancing demands for such funding through school clusters is an aspect of Chapter 4, 'Funding through school clusters: self-interest and co-operativeness'.

Checks and balances

Indications of (perhaps creative) tensions in the systems associated with special education and the various understandings of inclusion are those relating to the respective views and powers of parents, LEAs and schools and the potential for appeal to the Special Educational Needs and Disability Tribunal. Accordingly, in Chapter 5, 'Parents, local education authority and the Special Educational Needs and Disability Tribunal: balance of power', the relative power of parents, the LEA and the SENDIST are examined.

Another area for dealing with differing views and perspectives is that of the forum. In Chapter 6, 'The Special Educational Needs Forum: representation', the potential influence on policy and on other matters of participants in an SEN forum are considered.

The 'right' to inclusion

The final two chapters relate to the education of pupils with SEN, but in rather different ways. Chapter 7, 'Educating pupils with profound and multiple learning difficulties: rationality and autonomy', examines a moral position from which parents (and educators) compensate for gaps in liberal theory which is weak in offering protection to people with PMLD. This could be regarded as an example of including pupils in the process of education without specifying whether, or to what degree, this relates to mainstream or special schooling.

The balance of rights and duties in that aspect of inclusion concerned with the relative proportion of pupils in mainstream and special schools is considered in Chapter 8, 'Including pupils with SEN: rights and duties'. This is a more procedural view of inclusion with a focus on the respective roles of mainstream and special schools.

The future of inclusion

The future of inclusion in relation to special education is likely to be influenced by many factors. Among these is the extent to which aspirations to include all (whatever this is specified to mean in different contexts) enhance or erode the knowledge and skills of those presently working with pupils with SEN and hence raise or lower the quality of teaching and learning for pupils with SEN. Another factor is likely to be the degree to which the perceived negative effects of labelling balance against the view that it is necessary to identify and assess pupils with SEN. Appeals tribunals and representational foras are likely to be the arenas in which some of these tensions are worked through and perhaps worked out.

Finally, an important factor will be the respective esteem society places upon the value and functions of mainstream and special schools for pupils with the most severe and complex SEN.

2

Defining SEN: Distinguishing Goal-related Need and Unconditional Need

INTRODUCTION

Seeking to define a term is not always met with approval. Flann O'Brien observed that 'so long as there are people in the world, they will publish dictionaries defining what is unknown in terms of something equally unknown'.

This chapter considers the importance – to the local education authority, schools, parents and others – of agreeing how they will define SEN. It relates this to the importance of distinguishing between goal-related needs and unconditional needs.

The chapter sets the scene for considering these two understandings of 'need' by first looking at former categories of handicap used in England and at some criticisms of categories. It then examines the current legal definition of SEN in England and the notions of goal-directed and unconditional 'need' before focusing on the meaning of each of these kinds of need in relation to SEN.

I look at the implications of a continuum of SEN and non-normative SEN, suggesting that in both cases unconditional need might be mistaken for goal-related need, with its implications of 'justifiable compulsion', and that this can lead to an over-expansion of SEN provision.

As a corrective to the potential for the 'needs' in SEN to over-expand, along with associated provision, the importance of defining SEN is emphasised. I provide some possible responses to the earlier criticisms of categories. The related matters of 'areas of need' (in the Special Educational Needs Code of Practice (DfES 2001b)), categories (in the pupil-level annual census (DfES 2003a)) and locally agreed criteria are discussed as a continuing attempt to refine definitions of SEN.

A case study illustrates the efforts of an LEA in developing definitions of SEN. This is important, generally and in particular, in order to avoid inequitable funding.

The purpose of clear definitions of SEN

Where an area of human activity is difficult to describe and reach agreement about (as with SEN) and where it is also associated with extra funding and other preferential provision (as particularly in the case of School Action Plus and statements of SEN) it is essential that all involved agree when such provision is justified. This is not, of course, about providing more money for SEN, as if the issue would disappear if another £100 million were spent. It is about – whatever the budget for SEN is – allocating funding equitably and fairly. Without criteria relating to what SEN is, such fairness and attempts at equity are elusive and any system lies open to abuse.

The point of developing and maintaining local agreement on definitions of SEN is perhaps best indicated where an LEA and its partners have not done this. It is then open to schools seeking to maximise their income, particularly vocal lobby groups and especially articulate and concerned parents who can spend time on the activity to create their own versions of what SEN might be. Such groups may then press the LEA, particularly with regard to the statutory assessment of pupils, to concur with their perspective and appeal to the SEN and Disability Tribunal if they do not.

Former categories of handicap in England and Wales and criticisms of categories

Before the notion of SEN was developed in England and Wales, 'handicaps' were understood according to categories. Official 'categories' of handicap in England and Wales (outlined, for example, in Brennan 1982) were:

- blind/partially sighted;
- deaf/partially hearing;
- physically handicapped/delicate;
- maladjusted;
- educationally subnormal (severe);
- educationally subnormal (moderate);
- speech defect; and
- epileptic.

These categories represented the developmental dimension – such as sight, hearing or cognition – most obviously impaired. Among the criticisms of such categories (see also Frederickson and Cline 2002: 100–1) are that they can be restrictive, demeaning, oversimplifying and pathologising, as indicated below:

1   If a child is understood merely in terms of a category of disability or learning difficulty, this could be misleadingly restrictive because other developmental dimensions may be affected that are not covered by the category.

2   If a child is understood merely in terms of a category of disability or learning difficulty, this could be demeaning because it appears to place a greater emphasis on the difficulty/disability than on the child.

3   Categories can oversimplify a child's complexity because an individual pupil's particular pattern of strengths and weakness may be more complex than is suggested by a category relating to disabilities and learning difficulties.

4   Categories pathologise individual children by giving insufficient emphasis to the effect of the child's environment which may exacerbate or ameliorate the child's difficulty/disability.

In England and Wales, such criticisms led to the concept of 'categories of handicap' being replaced by 'special educational needs' (SEN) following the Warnock Report of 1978 (Department of Education and Science 1978). The notion of SEN entered legislation in the Education Act 1981 and the same definition has been passed into subsequent Acts, being currently part of the Education Act 1996.

Categories of handicap described about 2 per cent of the school population and applied to pupils usually in special schools. But the new term SEN was meant to apply to about one in six children at any one time and to about 20 per cent of the school population if a child's whole school career was considered.

Special educational needs

Partly in response to criticisms of categories, the concept of SEN was introduced in England. Under the Education Act 1996, section 312, children have SEN if they have a learning difficulty which calls for special educational provision to be made for them. Children have a learning difficulty if they:

(a)   have a significantly greater difficulty in learning than the majority of children of the same age;

(b)   have a disability which either prevents or hinders them from making use of educational facilities of a kind generally provided for children of the same age in schools within the area of the local education authority; or

(c)   are under the compulsory school age and fall within the definition at paragraph (a) and (b) above, or would do so if special educational provision were not made for them.

Special educational provision means:

(a) for children age 2 or over, educational provision which is additional to, or otherwise different from, the educational provision made generally for children of their age in schools maintained by the LEA (other than special schools) in the area, and

(b) for children under 2 years, educational provision of any kind.

The definition has a layered structure. A child may have a 'difficulty in learning' but this may not be significantly greater than the majority of children of the same age. If it is, then it is considered a 'learning difficulty'. If the learning difficulty 'calls for' special educational provision to be made that is, as defined, 'additional to, or otherwise different from' normal provision, then it constitutes an SEN.

Similarly, a child may have a 'disability' but the disability may not 'prevent or hinder' in the way defined in the Act. If it does, then it is considered a 'learning difficulty'. If the learning difficulty 'calls for' special educational provision to be made, as defined, then it is considered an SEN.

Goal-related need and unconditional need

A key aspect of the term, 'special educational need' is, of course, 'need' itself. To begin to clarify the concept of 'need' one may begin by comparing and contrasting it with the notion of 'want'. In certain contexts, the terms 'need' and 'want' can be used almost interchangeably. The concept of 'need' can convey standing in want of something. Indeed the word 'want' is sometimes used, when speaking of poverty, interchangeably with 'need'. People who are very poor may be 'in want' or 'in need' or 'needy'. It will be remembered that Dickens, in *A Christmas Carol*, has the Ghost of Christmas Present reveal to Scrooge the wretched child figures of 'Ignorance' and 'Want'.

But 'need' can also be used in a different way to 'want'. To 'want' something implies a desire to have something, perhaps property. I might want a second (or third) car but I cannot be said to 'need' it in the same way that I might 'need' one car to travel to a place of work that is poorly served by public transport.

The expression 'need' can be used in a way that necessitates a particular goal and also in a way that may not. Consider the first sense in which 'need' implies seeking a certain goal. In such cases, an action 'needs' to be performed or a situation requires some course of action. For something to be 'needful', it is required for a purpose. If I say I need something, there is an implied notion that I need it for a purpose. The purpose may be trivial as when I, say, need a ladder in order to clean cobwebs from the ceiling. In such an instance the use of the term 'need' seems quite in order so long as the person I am addressing understands the context. On the other hand, the purpose may be serious, as when I say I need air in order to breathe or I need water in order to survive. In both the trivial and the serious cases just suggested one is making a conditional assertion of need. Such instances may be paraphrased: 'I need X if I am to achieve Y'. The goal may be trivial or serious. If the goal is serious, as in 'I need water in order to survive', there is an implication that there is a justifiable obligation to provide for it.

Suppose a parent says that his child 'needs' extra tuition (paid by the state through taxes). To understand what is being said, we may need to know that there is an unmentioned clause: '... if he is to get a place in the best university'. Once this unmentioned clause is made explicit, there is then room for the question of whether this is a worthwhile goal and whether, for example, the state has any obligation to help him achieve it.

However, there are ways in which the term 'need' is used in which the assertion of need is not so clearly relative to a project. For example, when one speaks of 'special educational need' in an educational context, the assertion is not made relative to some goal. Part of the force of the term 'special educational needs' is the indication that there are no further questions to be asked in relation to goals or whether they are justified or whether it is justifiable for the state to provide. The demand is evident (whether or not it can be met) and the demand is not conditional on anything. Furthermore, in such circumstances 'need' can be taken (incorrectly) to signify being under an obligation as in the goal-related sense of the word 'need'.

The term 'need' can be used in a goal-directed sense. But it can also be used in an unconditional way that does not specify a particular goal. In the latter case, the term 'need' may appear to imply a justifiable obligation on the part of other people or of society when it is in fact debatable whether there is a justifiable obligation at all.

This leaves open the difficult question of how it is decided whether or not there is a justifiable demand or obligation in a particular case. But at least it does not seal off the question before it is even asked.

Goal-related need and SEN

When one speaks of severe SEN, the 'justifiable obligation' element of 'need' is often clear as in the following examples where the goal of the 'need' is explicit:

- A child who is blind may need to learn Braille in order to read.
- A child who is deaf may need early help and support with communication in order to communicate effectively.
- A child who has profound and multiple learning difficulties may need a 'small steps' curriculum and finely graded assessment in order to progress and have that progress recognised.
- A child with dyslexia may need 'scaffolding', such as writing frames and perhaps more time than pupils of the same age in order to write legibly and spell accurately.

But with less severe SEN the position is less clear. If a child is said to 'need' speech and language therapy because he has an SEN, what does this mean? It may mean that he 'needs' speech and language therapy in order to make better progress than he otherwise might, but this could apply to any child.

Almost any child, if given speech and language therapy, would make better progress in acquiring speech and language in part because of the one-to-one work that is often involved. So to say that a child 'needs' speech and language therapy must mean more than that the child would make better progress with such provision than he otherwise might.

What is usually implied is that the child is behind other children in the acquisition of speech and language and that, without the provision of speech and language therapy, the child may remain so or fall even further behind (or the child has a physical disability that will so obviously lead to falling behind if nothing is done that provision is given pre-emptively). This indicates the importance of information relating to the child's relative progress and attainment regarding (in the present example) speech and language acquisition compared with other children of the same age.

Unconditional need and SEN

If a parent wants more resources for his child's education, he can use the word 'need' loosely (and in the unconditional sense) to express this, but can suggest that there is a 'justifiable obligation', as might be the case if the need was goal-related. If such terminology is used loosely, the case for extra resources may seem more compelling than it really is. Coupled with the fundamental principle of the *Special Educational Needs Code of Practice* (Department for Education and Skills 2001b, chapter 1, section 5) that 'a child with special educational needs should have their needs met', the case could seem even more justifiable.

For someone to say that a child claimed to have SEN 'needs' certain provision without specifying the goal of the 'need' ('she needs this in order to') can pre-empt the question of whether the provision is necessary or justifiable educationally or financially. In this context, confusion between goal-related and unconditional need can contribute to the over-expansion of the number of pupils considered to have SEN.

A further difficulty is that it is not always clear what it would mean to 'meet' or 'satisfy' an SEN, nor what would be achieved when the 'need' is met. What happens in practice may reflect a circular argument. A child who is considered to have SEN may be said to 'need' provision including (perhaps individual) specialised teaching. Her 'needs' will be met when this specialised teaching is provided. The goal in such an instance is about providing support. But to be justifiable, the goal should relate to the reason why the support is provided, for example to improve a child's reading level when it is considerably behind that of children of the same age.

'Unconditional need' appearing as 'goal-related need' implying justifiable compulsion

There are opportunities in special education for 'need' to be presented in such a way that it may be taken to be goal-related when it is in fact unconditional and when there may be no justifiable compulsion to provide extra resources. These opportunities are evident in relation to continua and SEN and to so-called non-normative conditions.

Continua and SEN

The *Special Educational Needs Code of Practice* (Department for Education and Skills 2001b, chapter 1, section 37) envisages a range of strategies to meet a continuum of SEN:

> The Code advises the adoption of a range of strategies that recognise the various complexities of need, the different responsibilities to assess and meet those needs, and the associated range and variations in provision, which best reflect and promote common recognition of the continuum of special educational needs.

Envisaging a continuum of SEN can suggest a move away from an over-rigid approach to labelling. At its most constraining, labelling assumes SEN is predominantly within the child and suggests that the label completely describes a child. A continuum of 'need' suggests that at some point the 'need' part of the continuum merges into a part in which children do not have learning 'needs'. This suggests that children with SEN do not differ qualitatively from other children, but only in quantitative degree of disability or difficulty. However, there may effectively be qualitative differences, as when a child is blind or deaf or has no limbs. It would be odd to say that a child who is blind is on a continuum of children who have sight. The difference in degree of having sight and being legally blind is so great that it becomes effectively qualitative.

This supposed continuum of SEN has led to some previous 'categories' also being considered as continua and therefore becoming ever wider. For example, in England, the former category of 'maladjusted' was itself difficult enough to define. It became, first, 'emotional and behavioural difficulties', and then an 'area' of 'behavioural, emotional and social difficulties' which has extended to include attention deficit hyperactivity disorder. Autism was not previously a category but became accepted as a distinct condition relating to communication and interaction. It is now considered part of a wider conception of autistic spectrum disorder.

Consequently, post-Warnock, not only is the definition of SEN ten times wider (2% to 20%) than the previous categories of handicap, but the 'areas' of SEN are widening too.

Normative and non-normative conditions

Normative conditions are those for which there are widely accepted 'norms' or measures that are related to the wider population of children. So, given that there are certain 'norms' concerning the usual range and acuity of eyesight under specified conditions, these can be used to specify that a child has a visual impairment or is blind. Similarly, there are norms relating to hearing ability so that where a child falls outside these norms in specified conditions, it may be said that he has hearing impairment or is deaf. Medical diagnoses exist regarding epilepsy. Standardised tests, including tests for intelligence and attainment, can help identify that a child has profound and multiple learning difficulties or severe learning difficulties. Severe speech and language difficulties are assessed using standardised tests allowing comparisons with the development of other children.

Justifiable concerns have been raised about non-normative conditions (Tomlinson 1982). With such conditions, it is not possible to make clear comparisons with other children in the same way. It is not easy to distinguish pupils considered to have moderate learning difficulties from other children who may not be considered to have such difficulties but who may not be attaining as well as many other children. Less severe emotional and behavioural difficulties are difficult to determine because the context of the school and the skills of particular teachers in managing the difficult behaviour that may be associated with social, emotional and behavioural difficulties (SEBD) are so important. The range within which restlessness and poor concentration justify a judgement that a child has attention deficit hyperactivity disorder are difficult to identify. At what sort of level clumsiness and poor co-ordination warrant a 'diagnosis' of dyspraxia is open to debate. Non-normative conditions are, consequently, particularly difficult to define. This can lead to increasingly wider identification justified as rectifying previously unsatisfactory 'diagnosis'.

It will be seen that this difficulty of defining non-normative SEN also relates to the notion of a continuum of SEN discussed earlier. Where there is a continuum, any suggestion that there might be an agreed cut-off point (or 'band') where a child can be considered to have SEN becomes harder to justify. For example, the point where a child is considered slightly less well co-ordinated than other children and where he might be considered 'dyspraxic' becomes a matter of careful judgement.

The importance of defining SEN

Given the difficulties that emerge when using the term 'need', it may not be surprising that attempts to define SEN more closely remain important. The continuing use and refinement of categories and areas of need indicate this. Indeed, the criticisms that have been made of categories have not diminished their importance, although they have, sometimes rightly, indicated the disadvantages of viewing categories too rigidly.

Responding to criticisms of categories

The criticisms of categories noted earlier may be addressed to some degree and will now be reconsidered. It will be remembered that categories could be considered restrictive, demeaning, oversimplifying and pathologising.

First, if a child is understood merely in terms of a category of disability or learning difficulty, this could be misleadingly restrictive because other developmental dimensions may be affected that are not covered by the category. This is true in some instances. But it may not be necessary to seek to understand the child merely in terms of categories but only partly in terms of categorical descriptions and then only in relation to education. For example, if one considers pupils with severe behavioural, emotional and social difficulties, such pupils can make good personal, social and academic progress in safe and emotionally secure provision with such features as very small class sizes and the opportunity for counselling. There do not often appear to be other difficulties that would educationally override the view (and the evidence) that such provision helps such pupils emotionally, socially and educationally.

Even where there are several areas of disability or learning difficulty, it often makes sense from an educational point of view to consider one area as the 'main' area of disability / learning difficulty. For example, where a pupil has profound and multiple learning difficulties, it is, educationally, of primary importance that a curriculum is provided that is graded into very small steps so that progress can be made and recognised.

Secondly, if a child is understood merely in terms of a category of disability or learning difficulty, this could be demeaning because it appears to place a greater emphasis on the difficulty / disability than the child.

It can be just as difficult to ensure that a child is not considered only in terms of a category of disability or learning difficulty as it is to ensure that the same child is not regarded solely in terms of having SEN. If this is so, then the effect of the Warnock Report (Department of Education and Science 1978) could have been to inadvertently shift the perceived limitations of labelling, from a small percentage of children to around a fifth of all children.

But even if one recognises some validity in the view that categories of disability and learning difficulty can have a potentially distorting effect, it seems possible to recognise the child's difficulty or disability and not assume that this says everything that there is to be said about the child. It is only in the educational sense that sufficient recognition has to be made of the child's SEN to ensure that suitable provision is made.

Thirdly, categories can oversimplify a child's complexity because an individual pupil's particular pattern of strengths and weaknesses may be more complex than is suggested by a category relating to disabilities and learning difficulties.

This is true in some instances and should be fundamental to any teacher's interaction with her class. The question is whether, as a starting point, the notion of a category is helpful educationally. If it is, then this does not prevent further information about the child's learning strengths and weaknesses being used within any particular educational setting such as a mainstream or special school.

Last, categories pathologise individual children by giving insufficient emphasis to the effect of the child's environment, which may exacerbate or ameliorate the child's difficulty / disability.

When this view is expressed, the environment to which reference is being made is usually the home or the community and it is important that the impact of the child's environment in this sense is taken into account.

Clearly, if a child has unfortunate home circumstances, this may have an impact of her educational progress, but it does not absolve the teacher and others from recognising when a child's progress is causing concern and identifying the child and acting to improve the child's progress.

However, an important aspect of the work of educators is to create a teaching environment in which effective learning takes place. The judgement about a child's difficulty / disability is taken in the context of this learning environment and a judgement about whether or not a child has SEN is an educational judgement, largely related to the progress or lack of progress that the child is making.

Educators have to be vigilant that categorical thinking does not lead to an underestimating of the importance of adjusting and modifying the environment, even in small ways, to aid learning.

SEN Code

The *Special Educational Needs Code of Practice* is careful to avoid indicating that SEN is exclusively 'within' the child, but that it involves an interaction between the environment and the child. This is particularly expressed in terms of attainment and progress, teaching and learning as is evident in Chapters 4 through 6 of the Code dealing respectively with:

- Early Years Action and Early Years Action Plus;
- School Action and School Action Plus in the primary phase; and
- School Action and School Action Plus in the secondary sector.

For example, in early education settings, SEN is related closely to 'inadequate' progress, making it necessary to take some 'additional or different action to enable the child to *learn more effectively* (4.13, italics added). In the primary phase, it is noted that assessment, which may lead to a judgement that a child has SEN should be fourfold. 'It should focus on the child's learning characteristics, the learning environment that the school is providing for the child, the task and the teaching style' (5.6). In the secondary sector, progress is emphasised (e.g. 6.12 and 6.51).

The importance of 'areas of need' is evident in the Code. In a chapter providing guidance on the statutory assessment of SEN, the Code maintains that it 'does not assume that there are hard and fast categories' of SEN (7.52). It recognises that each child is 'unique'. It continues: 'there is a wide spectrum of special educational needs that are frequently interrelated, although there are also specific needs that usually relate directly to particular types of impairment'.

Also, 'Children will have needs and requirements which may fall into at least one of four areas, many children will have interrelated needs. The impact of these combinations on the child's ability to function, learn and succeed should be taken into account' (7.52). The Code continues to seek a balance between using categorical language and expressing caution, stating 'Although needs and requirements can usefully be organised into areas, individual pupils may well have needs which span two or more areas' (7.53).

The areas of need (7.52) are:

- communication and interaction;
- cognition and learning;
- behaviour, emotional and social development; and
- sensory and/or physical.

The range of difficulties considered relating to 'communication and interaction' will include children with speech and language impairments or disorders, specific learning difficulties, hearing impairments and 'those who demonstrate features within the autistic spectrum' (7.55). Cognition and learning will include children who 'demonstrate features of' specific, moderate, severe, profound learning difficulties (7.58). Behavioural, emotional and social development includes children who are hyperactive and lack concentration as well as those who 'demonstrate features of' emotional and behavioural difficulties and others (7.60). Sensory and/or physical needs are considered to comprise 'a wide spectrum of sensory, multi-sensory and physical difficulties' (7.62). These extend from 'profound and permanent deafness or visual impairment to lesser levels of loss, which may only be temporary', and other difficulties (7.62).

Pupil Level Annual Schools Census categories

Also, the Department for Education and Skills (2003a) required from January 2004 the Pupil Level Annual Schools Census (PLASC) to be in categories. The 'areas' of need have been subdivided into 'the categories used by Ofsted' (ibid. p.1). These are:

- Cognition and learning needs
  - Specific learning difficulty (SpLD)

- Moderate learning difficulty (MLD)
- Severe learning difficulty (SLD)
- Profound and multiple learning difficulty (PMLD)
- Behaviour, emotional and social development needs
  - Behaviour, emotional and social difficulty
- Communication and interaction needs
  - Speech, language and communication needs (SLCN)
  - Autistic spectrum disorder (ASD)
- Sensory and/or physical needs
  - Visual impairment (VI)
  - Hearing impairment (HI)
  - Multisensory impairment (MSI)
  - Physical disability (PD)
- Other (OTH)

The guidance states that, 'We are aware that many pupils have more than one type of difficulty. We are therefore asking you to record information on pupils' greatest or primary need and, where appropriate, their secondary need'. Data on the type of difficulty is required only for pupils on Early Years Action Plus, School Action Plus or those having a statement of SEN. Descriptions of each of these categories is provided in the guidance.

Definitions of SEN

While categories and areas of need are aspects of definitions of SEN, they are only part of the picture. Some LEAs further refine the areas and categories so that there is the opportunity to develop local agreement about what SEN might mean. The reasons such agreements and definitions are developed locally relate to the legal definition of SEN.

It will be remembered that under the Education Act 1996, section 312, children have SEN if they have a learning difficulty which calls for special educational provision to be made for them. Part of the definition of learning difficulty is that children have a learning difficulty if they 'have a significantly greater difficulty in learning than the majority of children of the same age' or 'have a disability which either prevents or hinders them from making use of educational facilities of a kind generally provided for children of the same age in schools within the area of the local education authority'.

Part of the definition of special educational provision is that, for children aged 2 or over, it is 'educational provision which is additional to, or otherwise different from, the educational provision made generally for children of their age in schools maintained by the LEA (other than special schools) in the area'.

Consequently, in the absence of national guidance about the level of 'difficulty in learning' that might constitute a 'learning difficulty' perhaps requiring special educational provision, LEAs tend to develop their own definitions. Also, with regard to the level of disability that constitutes a 'learning difficulty' that may require special educational provision, the level is in part determined by the local level of provision.

Case study: Blackpool Local Education Authority and developing definitions in SEN

Blackpool Borough Council Education and Cultural Services Department, in its 'Guidance on Meeting Special Educational Needs and the Effective Use of Resources' (revised edition April 2002) indicates its approach to the delegation of funds to schools. This was developed from a model initiated in Oldham some years previously. Essentially, the LEA delegates funds to schools for high-incidence SEN such as moderate learning difficulty, specific learning difficulty and emotional and behavioural difficulty. This funding is calculated using:

(a) for primary schools, a baseline element and an indicator of the eligibility of pupils for free school meals;

(b) for secondary schools, a baseline element, an indicator of the eligibility of pupils for free school meals, and information from cognitive ability test (CAT) scores.

The LEA retains funds for low-incidence SEN such as physical disability, sensory difficulties and profound and multiple learning difficulties and for pupils with statements who are new to the area.

A panel for statutory assessment moderation (PSAM Training Pack, 2002–3) advises the Assistant Director (Pupil Support) on whether evidence submitted with a request for statutory assessment of SEN meets locally published criteria. PSAM meets every four weeks and includes LEA officers, three head teachers and two SENCOs. There are five criteria that have been developed by members of the PSAM group and endorsed by the local Joint Steering Group of head teachers. It is considered important that the guidelines are adhered to to ensure that the process is equitable and to assist the PSAM group in carrying out its function. The criteria are:

(a) Present detailed documented records to show that all reasonable steps have been taken to meet the pupil's needs using the totality of the school's own delegated resources.

(b) Provide an account of the co-ordinated involvement of appropriate, centrally held LEA support agencies.

(c) Provide evidence that the pupil's needs cannot be met by a combination of the school's own resources and the resources held centrally which are available without a statement.

(d) Demonstrate that the pupil's needs are 'exceptional', i.e. significantly greater than other pupils of the same age in the borough.

(e) Demonstrate that the pupil's needs are severe and complex and have highly specialised and long-term implications.

With reference to criteria (d) and (e), there are published 'indicators' for statutory assessment (PSAM Training Materials 2000) that the child's needs are 'exceptional' and 'severe and complex', examples of which are given below.

General learning difficulties

For children below Key Stage 2, severity is measured by assessing the child's cognitive ability. It will be appropriate to consider statutory assessment if:

- there is evidence that the child's cognitive ability is at or below the first centile on an appropriate test of general intellectual ability (that is, only 1 per cent of children of the same age would score lower); or
- there is evidence that the child is not progressing through the curriculum (i.e. is below level 1 of the National Curriculum).

For children at Key Stage 2 and above, the level of severity is measured by the pupil's attainments. It will be appropriate to consider statutory assessment if:

- attainments in **either** reading, spelling or number are at or below the first centile on appropriate standardised tests;
- attainments in reading, spelling and number are **all** at or below the second centile on appropriate standardised tests.

Guidelines for ceasing a statement for general learning difficulties are when a pupil reaches attainments in literacy and numeracy that are consistently above the fifth centile.

Specific learning difficulty

It will be appropriate to consider statutory assessment if the following criteria are **all** present:

- reading age less than 9 years;
- reading centile below 20;
- discrepancy between reading ability and reading level predicted by intelligence quotient is at or below the first centile (that only 1 per cent of pupils of the same age are likely to have such a large discrepancy between their attainment and the attainment predicted by IQ test).

Guidelines for ceasing a statement of SEN for a pupil with specific learning difficulty is when:

- the pupil has a reading age of 9 years 6 months;
- spelling and/or mathematics attainment is above 8 years 6 months.

It will be seen from the case study indicators for specific learning difficulties which really relate to dyslexia developed by Blackpool that it has sought to avoid a potential problem with a 'deficit' model. This is that, if one allows such a model to be taken too far, it becomes possible to envisage statutory assessment and the possibility of a statement of SEN for a child who can read as well as others of the same age. This arises because the supposed 'discrepancy' between what the child is attaining and what the IQ test suggests he should attain might exist if a child has a very high IQ suggesting he should be reading well above age average and yet is 'only' attaining at age-average level. Blackpool, surely correctly, avoids this potential misdirection of SEN funds by specifying that other indicators should be present that relate to the child being behind other children of the same age in reading (i.e. reading centile below 20).

Blackpool has also developed indicators in relation to hearing impairment, visual impairment, physical difficulties, speech and language difficulties, autistic spectrum difficulties and emotional and behavioural difficulties. Some of these have a subjective element especially where the SEN is particularly difficult to define. For example, the indicators for emotional and behavioural difficulty include a consideration of such 'key issues' as the 'extent to which the pupil is preventing others from benefiting from the curriculum'. These are, in turn, assessed in terms of severity indications of the 'nature, frequency and severity of the problem' (PSAM Training Materials 2000).

Summary/conclusion

This chapter considered the importance, to the local education authority, schools, parents and others of agreeing how they will define SEN. It suggested that mistaking unconditional needs (such as special educational needs) for goal-related needs is likely to contribute to the inappropriate expansion of SEN. The related matters of 'areas of need' and categories were seen as a continuing attempt to refine definitions of SEN. Locally agreeing definitions of SEN is important in identifying and assessing pupils with SEN and avoiding inequitable funding.

3

School Equal Opportunity Policies: Equality and Discrimination

INTRODUCTION

George Orwell captured one of the dilemmas of striving for equality famously in Animal Farm, when the situation arises in which 'All animals are equal but some animals are more equal than others'. Certainly, real difficulties surround notions of equality. Reflecting this, written school policies may be based on a view of equal opportunities that make assumptions that do not take enough account of dilemmas regarding equality and discrimination. This chapter considers difficulties with the concept of equality. This leads to a consideration of the contested nature of the concept of equality of opportunity. I examine problems relating to definitions of discrimination which seek to link it to ideas of not allowing people's lives to be affected by circumstances not under their control. A further definition of discrimination is considered relating it to treating people with undeserved contempt, but this is also considered to have drawbacks. A position is commended which suggests that one should seek for others to be in a good enough position, not necessarily being equal, although further difficulties arise in determining what is 'good enough'.

In the light of this, the definition of discrimination in the Special Educational Needs and Disability Act 2001 (SENDA) is considered. The implications of the issues discussed in the chapter for school policies for pupils with SEN and equal opportunities are examined.

Underlying such policies appears to be the principle of treating children unequally (that is treating pupils with SEN preferentially). This is justified because of the difficulties and disabilities that pupils with SEN experience. This relates to the issue that, educationally, pupils with SEN are likely to require preferential treatment to move nearer to a position in which they can more equally benefit from the opportunities of which other children can more easily take advantage.

A case study presents a school's policies relating to equal opportunities with particular reference to sections on SEN.

School equal opportunities policies

School's written policies on equal opportunities often include references to 'equality' and 'discrimination' and statements asserting that the school seeks to offer 'equal opportunities' to pupils. The stated commitment to equal opportunities may be reinforced by some reference to groups of pupils who, it is thought, without special effort and care, may not always receive equal opportunities. These groups include girls and boys, pupils from different ethnic minority backgrounds and asylum seekers, as well as pupils with SEN.

The policy may also outline the strategies that the school adopts to try to ensure that the different groups of pupils have equal opportunities. These include gathering data on attainment for the groups and analysing these to see if there are discrepancies, and then seeking to explain them and develop strategies to minimise differences in attainment.

However, there are dilemmas concerning equality, equality of opportunity, and discrimination that are not always sufficiently recognised. Particular issues arise in relation to pupils with SEN. Is the notion of equality as straightforward as it appears? Is seeking equality of opportunity a legitimate or even a desirable aim? Is discrimination better understood as treating people unequally or as trying to ensure that all people are in a 'good enough' position? What is the Special Educational Needs and Disability Act's perspective on discrimination? What are the implications for school policy?

Equality

Egalitarianism, the view that society should be based on the principle of equal rights and opportunities for all, may start from a belief in equality. One example is that members of society are all equal in terms of some quality that each possesses, such as a common humanity. Another example is that our equality consists in our relations with each other, that is we are all partners in a common enterprise.

One attempt to find a common feature that justifies treating people equally concerns potential. The argument is that there is a gap between what one can achieve unaided, when provided only with basic necessities such as food and shelter, and what one can achieve given the best education and support. Because this gap in potential is universal (although the size of the gap varies), it may be taken as an aspect of humanity shared by everyone and therefore a justification for treating people equally in the distribution of resources.

Such a view is not universally accepted. For example, Cavanagh (2002: 110) maintains that such similarities are not sufficiently detached from differences (the fact that the gap is even bigger for some people than for others) to make a convincing case for preferring to emphasise the similarity rather than the difference.

Therefore the notion of equality is rejected. Such considerations as the difficulties in justifying seeking equality may lead egalitarians and others to move from arguing for equality to supporting equality of opportunity.

Equality of opportunity as a contested concept

In considering equality of opportunity, a useful starting point is to recognise that the notion itself is contested. There are theories that argue in support of an egalitarian society, caution against social inequality and which would support an approach aiming for equality of opportunity. For example, the 'justice as fairness' theory put forward by Rawls (1971) uses principles that, it is argued, people would endorse if they were deprived of knowledge of their own social status and position. In a hypothetical situation in which someone is deprived of any knowledge about their own abilities, should that person be given a choice of whether to live in an egalitarian society or an inegalitarian one, he would be likely to choose to live in a egalitarian society. One reason is that the hope of being rich would be countered by the fear of being poor, persuading the person behind the veil of ignorance about his own abilities to choose a society that is 'fair' (ibid.: 148).

Accordingly, social inequality, in the sense of different treatment, is justified only when it has the effect of benefiting the least advantaged by improving incentives and increasing the size of the social pot. People co-operating for mutual advantage are entitled to equal claims for the results of their co-operation. They should not be penalised because of factors over which they have no control such as genetic inheritance (or race or gender). Redistribution is a 'just' procedure because it conforms to a widely held view of what is fair. Equality of opportunity may be justified similarly.

However, other theories challenge the whole approach of equal opportunities which is considered to violate property rights and compromise freedom. An example is Nozick's (1974) 'rights' view of social justice and of equality of opportunity. This follows from his essentially libertarian conception of the state. Nozick seeks to demonstrate that an 'ultra minimal' state (having a monopoly over the use of force in a territory) emerges from a system of 'private protection associations'. The ultra minimal state is transformed into a 'minimal' state which involves redistribution for the 'general provision' of protective services (ibid.: 52). The transitions leading from the state of nature to the ultra minimal state to the minimal state are morally legitimate and the minimal state itself is morally legitimate, Nozick argues.

The transition from private protection agencies to the ultra minimal state will occur by an 'invisible hand process' in a way that is morally permissible and does not violate anyone's property rights as understood in this conception of social justice. The transition from ultra minimal state to minimal state morally 'must occur'. It would not be morally permissible for individuals to keep the monopoly in the ultra minimal state without providing protective services for everyone even if this requires specific redistribution (ibid.: 113–19).

No state more powerful or more extensive than the minimal state is legitimate or justifiable. Therefore such developments as 'social justice / redistributive justice' and 'equality of opportunity', which go further than the minimal state, are neither legitimate nor justifiable. Consequently, Nozick sees justice in entitlement terms, that is not as about equality but as about individual property rights. Someone acquiring a 'holding' (property) in accordance with, 'the principle of justice in acquisition' is entitled to the holding. Someone acquiring a holding in accordance with 'the principle of justice in transfer' from someone else who is entitled to that holding is entitled to the holding (ibid.: 150).

'Justice as fairness' views assume that everyone has some entitlement on the totality of natural assets as a 'pool', with no one having differential claims. The distribution of natural abilities is seen as a collective asset. Nozick accepts that in a free society people's talents do benefit others and not just themselves. What he questions is the extracting of even more benefit to others, suggesting that envy underlies this conception of justice (ibid.: 229).

Nozick maintains that there are two ways to achieve equality of opportunity: the first is to deliberately worsen the circumstances of those who are better favoured with opportunity; the second is to improve the situation of those who are less well favoured. The second approach requires resources and, as these have to come from somewhere, this implies that someone else will have to accept a worse situation. Because the holding of others may not be seized, people must be convinced to choose to give some of their holding to help achieve greater equality of opportunity. (This may be in the form of charitable giving or in the form of taxes for which the population may have voted.)

There is no social obligation to try to 'rectify' inequalities. 'Equal opportunities' violates individual property rights and compromises freedom. The main objection to considering everyone as having a right to such things as equality of opportunity, and enforcing that right, is 'that these "rights" require a substructure of things and materials and actions; and other people may have rights and entitlements over these' (ibid.: 238).

Such, in essence, are the views of Rawls and of Nozick. What tends to happen in practice is that a liberal democracy steers a middle course between these two positions. It is important, however, to remember that 'equality of opportunity' is a contested value supported or not supported in varying measure by different members of society and in different degrees at different times. It is not a given good.

Discrimination and not allowing people's lives to be negatively affected by circumstances not under their control

If discrimination is defined in terms of equality and of equality of opportunity, and both of these notions are problematic, then arguing against discrimination as defined faces difficulties.

There is a negative (and difficult to sustain) view that people's lives should not be affected by anything that is not under their control. There also appears to be a growing tendency to combine the negative way of thinking about control (that is that people's lives should not be affected by what is not under their control) with a commitment to equality. This tends to lead to the unsustainable view that it is unfair for one person to have less than another through no fault of his own.

Discrimination may be thought of in vague terms. It may be 'bottom up', taking the view that people's prospects should not depend on disability. For example, schools should not intentionally discriminate on the grounds of disability. Alternatively, discrimination may be 'top down' so that no one should suffer because of their disability. For instance, there should be no correlation between disability and any kind of disadvantage. The use of such constructions can lead to the unsustainable view that both perspectives are concerned with 'discrimination'. So when considering discrimination, people may not have anyone's behaviour in mind. They may just mean that there is a correlation between being disabled and experiencing a certain kind of disadvantage.

People with physical disabilities experience certain disadvantages. Many aspects of life are more difficult for them, but not because anyone has deliberately constructed the environment to contain 'barriers' that will purposely make life more difficult for the disabled. Designers are not guilty of discrimination in the sense that they have not knowingly behaved in a discriminatory way towards someone who is disabled. Yet people try to articulate the point that life is more difficult for disabled people by saying that they suffer 'discrimination'.

This does not imply that it is not a positive aim to design and construct buildings that are accessible to people in wheelchairs. A building with access at least allows a person in a wheelchair a choice whether or not to use it. But where a building does not have such access, while it may be unfortunate, it is questionable whether the use of the term 'discrimination' is meaningful in the sense of active behaviour.

Discrimination as treating people with undeserved contempt and being in a 'good enough' position

There is another approach to discrimination which is not to regard it as linked to equality of opportunity, that is not treating people unequally. In this alternative view, discrimination is seen as treating people with contempt when it is not deserved (Cavanagh 2002). This leaves open the question of when contempt might be 'deserved' and what treating people who deserve contempt might entail. Another limitation of this understanding of discrimination is that it does not capture the differential aspect in treating one person in one way and one person in another way for reasons that are not justifiable.

Cavanagh maintains that, in addition to ensuring that there is no discrimination in terms of treating people with unjustifiable contempt, an effort should be made to ensure that no one is left without hope. Being left without hope is understood as leaving someone in a position in which they can do nothing to change their life for the better.

People's lives should be, to some extent, under their control. Therefore, we should be concerned if certain groups have bad prospects. This involves asking if people are in a good enough position, not asking whether they are equal.

This, in turn, leaves open the very difficult question of what is 'good enough' and who is to decide. It does, however, face squarely the impossibility of everyone being equal. It also recognises the dilemma that to offer equal opportunities to people who may find it difficult to take advantage of them is to offer the equal opportunity for everyone to be unequal. On the other hand, it also offers the opportunity for some people to move towards greater equality with others.

Discrimination in the Special Education Needs and Disability Act 2001 relating to children with disabilities (who may or may not have SEN) concerns the treatment of pupils in a much more 'bottom up' way. In this respect it is more pragmatic and justifiable than the approach of seeking to link 'discrimination' with not allowing people's lives to be negatively affected by circumstances not under their control. Neither does the Act suggest that all children and young people are equal. It is to this Act that the chapter now turns.

The Special Education Needs and Disability Act 2001 and discrimination

This section outlines the provisions of the Special Education Needs and Disability Act 2001 (SENDA) especially in relation to discrimination. The SENDA amends the Disability Discrimination Act 1995 and part 4 of the Education Act 1996 and makes further provision against discrimination on grounds of disability in schools and other educational establishments. The provisions of the SENDA concerning SEN apply to England and Wales. Provisions relating to the rights of disabled people in education affect England, Wales and Scotland (except the duty to produce an accessibility strategy or plan that does not apply to Scotland).

A Code of Practice concerning schools (Disability Rights Commission 2001a) and another Code of Practice for the post-16 sector (Disability Rights Commission 2001b) supplement the SENDA. The Act is in three parts. Part 1 of the SENDA amends the

Education Act 1996 for children with SEN. Part 3 concerns supplementary matters. The main part, as far as discrimination is concerned, is part 2.

Part 2 of the SENDA deals with disability discrimination in education. It places duties on further and higher education institutions and local education authorities (LEAs) with regard to adult education and youth services provision. It extends the role of the Disability Rights Commission and allows it to prepare new codes of practice explaining the legislation. The Disability Rights Commission may set up an independent conciliation service for disputes arising from schools' duties under the Act. Its purpose is to promote the settlement of claims without recourse to the SENDIST or other body. Both the parents and the 'responsible body' have to agree for disputes to be referred to conciliation.

It specifies what LEAs and schools (including independent schools and non-maintained special schools) in England and Wales must do. It also places duties on local authorities, independent schools, self-governing schools and grant-aided schools in Scotland. One such duty is not to treat a disabled pupil less favourably for a reason relating to his disability than someone to whom that reason does not apply, without justification. It is unlawful for the responsible body of a school (usually governors) to discriminate against a disabled child who might become a pupil at the school in relation to its admission arrangements, exclusions or in the education or associated services provided for or offered to pupils at the school.

Three aspects taken together constitute unlawful discrimination. These are that the less favourable treatment:

- is for a reason that is directly related to the child's disability;
- is less favourable treatment than someone gets if the reason does not apply to them; and
- cannot be justified.

Less favourable treatment may be justified if it is:

- the result of a permitted form of selection; or
- is for both a material and substantial reason.

A blanket policy is not considered a material and substantial reason because it takes no account of individual circumstances.

Another duty is to make reasonable adjustments to admission arrangements, exclusions and, in relation to education and related services, to ensure that disabled pupils (or prospective pupils) are not substantially disadvantaged in comparison with their non-disabled peers without justification. 'Reasonable adjustments' are not intended to require the responsible body to provide auxiliary aids and services. For schools in the public sector, these are made through the SEN framework for pupils whose disability leads to a learning difficulty calling for special educational provision to be made. Neither does the responsible body have to make physical alterations to the buildings. These are covered by the new planning duties. The SENDA duties are anticipatory in the sense that generally a school cannot wait until a disabled pupil arrives before making an adjustment. The only justification for not making a reasonable adjustment is that there is a material and substantial reason.

The SENDA sets out requirements (with regard to England and Wales) on LEAs and schools to draw up accessibility strategies (LEAs) and accessibility plans (schools) to improve access to education at schools over time. These strategies and plans have to address the following three elements of planned improvements in access for disabled pupils:

- improvements in access to the curriculum;

- physical improvements to increase access to education and associated services; and

- improvements in the provision of information in a range of formats for disabled people.

Under the planning duties, governing bodies must include information in their annual reports about the accessibility plan showing how they will increase access for disabled pupils to education at the school.

If parents consider that a responsible body has discriminated against their child, they can claim unlawful discrimination. The SENDIST may order any reasonable remedy except financial compensation. It hears claims relating to:

- fixed-period exclusions from all schools; and

- admissions to and permanent exclusions from all schools other than maintained schools and city academies.

Admissions appeals panels or exclusion appeals panels hear claims of unlawful discrimination regarding a refusal to admit to, and permanent exclusion from, maintained schools and city academies. An admissions appeal is made in compliance with a Code of Practice on Admission Appeals and the panel can order that a pupil be admitted. Exclusion appeals panels can order the pupil's reinstatement.

The approach of the SENDA to discrimination seeks to define the behaviour that can be considered unlawful discrimination under carefully prescribed conditions and recognises financial constraints.

Implications for school policies

Where equal opportunities approaches are applied to groups of pupils other than pupils with SEN, for example comparing girls and boys who do not have SEN, the initial assumption is that girls and boys are expected to achieve similarly in, say, mathematics. Therefore data on the relative attainment of boy and girls of the same age are compared, and if there are discrepancies, the school re-examines its practices to try to ensure that its own practices and expectations are not contributing to the difference. For example, if girls perform less well than boys, the school might consider if its staffing structure and expectations of girls, its resources, methods of teaching and other features are contributing to the lower performance of girls compared to boys. If such considerations indicate inequities, the school will seek to rectify such features, for example by ensuring that there are a range and variety of resources to cater for the expressed interests of boys and girls. Equality of opportunity in this context relates to removing supposed 'barriers' to the equal achievement of girls, such as uninteresting resources or lower expectations.

In relation to pupils with SEN there is an extra dimension. Consider pupils with a difficulty in learning that has led to a learning difficulty that calls for special educational provision and is therefore considered an SEN. For example, one may consider a pupil with profound learning difficulties. By definition, the attainment of the pupil will be below that of pupils of the same age. Given this, when a group of pupils with profound learning difficulties is compared with a group of pupils who do not have profound learning difficulties (or any difficulties in learning) a difference in attainment is expected. Indeed, if there were not a marked difference in attainment, one would question the notion that the first group of pupils had been correctly identified as having profound learning difficulties at all.

Therefore, the approach described earlier, that is used to seek to bring the attainment of boys and girls to similar levels, does not quite fit. While parents and teachers would accept that pupils with profound learning difficulties may make better progress in a good educational environment than a poor one, the expectation is not that their attainment will equal that of all pupils. Another way of suggesting this is that the notion of removing 'barriers' works to a certain degree but that teachers and others acknowledge that there is also a 'within child' element to the profound learning difficulty – for example, demonstrable physical damage to the brain.

Given this, if teachers and others are to be convinced that they are doing all that can be reasonably done to improve the attainment of a pupil with profound learning difficulties, then comparison is made with groups of other pupils with similar difficulties, for example in other schools. Consider, for example, two groups of pupils with profound learning difficulties starting from similar points (as indicated by baseline assessment) in two different schools. If these are compared, and one group does better than the other, the schools involved can begin to examine reasons why, in a similar way to that relating to possible differences between boys' attainment and girls' attainment outlined earlier.

Similar arguments apply if one is considering pupils with other SEN such as severe learning difficulties, specific learning difficulties and moderate learning difficulties.

In practice, with regard to pupils with SEN, mainstream schools are not pursuing equality for all pupils in the school, but are developing policy to explain and seek to justify preferential provision and funding for pupils with SEN. This unequal treatment is justified by assuming that the opportunities of pupils with SEN to benefit from education are being made more similar to those of pupils without SEN. In other words, an attempt is being made to reduce inequalities. This is expressed in terms of offering better opportunities through providing extra funding and support. This approach discriminates in favour of these pupils by providing the pupils with SEN with more resources and support than other children and young people.

Case study: extracts from an equal opportunities policy and an inclusion policy

Extracts below are taken from the 'Equal Opportunities and Racial Equality and Diversity Policy' and the 'Inclusion Policy' of the same school, a nursery and infant school. They are provided by kind permission of the school.

The establishment, which will be referred to as school X, has combined its formerly separate policies on 'Equality of opportunity' and 'Racial diversity' into a single policy, the Equal Opportunities and Racial Equality and Diversity Policy. Consequently, the extracts from this policy focus particularly on those aspects concerning, and illustrated by, reference to pupils with SEN.

The school's policy on Inclusion is wide and embraces, for example, ethnicity, gender and other features, as well as SEN. Again, aspects referring to pupils with SEN have been selected.

Although these extracts cannot convey the overarching intention of the policies, they do indicate the application of some of the terms that have been considered in this chapter. I have placed these terms in bold to demonstrate how they permeate the documents.

Equal Opportunities and Racial Equality and Diversity Policy

This policy is meant for the school community and others who want to know what they can expect from X Nursery and Infant School and how the school will tackle **discrimination** and promote **equality of opportunity** and good race relations. This policy has subsumed the school's policy for **Equality of Opportunity**.

Aims and objectives: equality opportunities: non-discriminatory

Not to **discriminate** against anyone, be they staff or pupil, on the grounds of their sex, race, colour, **disability**, religion, nationality, ethnic or national origins.

To promote the principles of **fairness and justice** for all through the education that we provide in our school.

To ensure that all pupils have **equal access** to the full range of educational **opportunities** provided by the school.

To constantly strive to remove any forms of indirect **discrimination** that may form barriers to learning.

The role of governors

The governing body has set out its commitment to **equal opportunities**, racial equality and diversity in this policy statement, and it will continue to do all it can to ensure that all members of the school community are treated fairly and with **equality**. An action plan, reviewed on an annual basis, is used to annually review provision and the success of the policy.

The governors take all reasonable steps to ensure that the school environment gives access to people with **disabilities**. The governing body will, in its annual report, record the arrangements made in the school for **disabled children**, staff and community members.

The governors welcome all applications to join the school, whatever background or **disability** a child may have.

The role of the head teacher

It is the head teacher's role to implement the school's **equal opportunities** and racial and diversity policy and s/he is supported by the governing body (e.g. through implementing the action plan and through monitoring) in so doing.

It is the head teacher's role to ensure that all staff is aware of the school policy on **equal opportunities**, racial and diversity, and that teachers and staff apply these guidelines fairly in all situations.

The head teacher promotes the principle of **equal opportunity** and racial and diversity **equality** when developing the curriculum and promotes respect for other people in all aspects of school life, for example in the assembly where respect for other people is a regular theme, and in displays shown around the school.

The role of the class teacher

The class teacher ensures that all children are treated **fairly**, **equally** and with respect. We do not **discriminate** against any child.

Monitoring and review

It is the responsibility of our governing body to monitor the effectiveness of this **Equal Opportunities**, Racial and Diversity Policy. The governing body does this by:

- monitoring the staff appointment process, so that no-one applying for a post at this school is **discriminated** against; requiring the head teacher to report to governors on an annual basis on the effectiveness of this policy;

- taking into serious consideration any complaints regarding **equal opportunity**, racial or diversity issues from parents, staff or children;

- ensuring that all policies work on line with the **Equal Opportunities**, Racial and Diversity Policy;

- implementing the **Equal Opportunities**, Racial and Diversity Action Plan.

Inclusion policy

Introduction

The mission statement of our school talks of valuing the individuality of all our children and that together we make a difference. We are committed to giving all our children every opportunity to achieve the highest standards. This policy helps to ensure that this happens for all the children in our school regardless of their age, gender, colour, race, **disability**, religion, nationality, attainment or background.

Aims and objectives

Our school aims to be an inclusive school. This means that **equality of opportunity** must be a reality for our children. We make this a reality through the attention we pay to the different groups of children within our school:

girls and boys;

minority ethnic and faith groups;

children who need support to learn English as an additional language;

children with **special educational needs**;

gifted and talented children; and

any children who are at risk of disaffection and exclusion.

The National Curriculum is our starting point for planning a curriculum that meets the specific needs of individuals and groups of children. We do this through:

responding to children's diverse learning needs;

setting suitable learning challenges;

overcoming potential barriers to learning and assessment for individuals and groups of pupils; and

providing other curricular **opportunities** outside the National Curriculum to meet the needs of individuals or groups of children. (This includes **speech and language therapy** and **mobility training**.)

Teaching and learning style

We aim to give all our children the **opportunity** to succeed and reach the highest level of personal achievement. When planning their work, teachers take into account the abilities of all their children. For some children we use the programmes of study from earlier key stages. This enables some of our children to make progress in their own lessons, perhaps after significant amounts of time spent away from school.

When the attainment of a child falls significantly below the expected level, teachers enable the child to succeed by planing work that is in line with that child's individual needs.

Teachers are familiar with the relevant **equal opportunities** legislation covering race, gender and **disability**.

Teachers ensure that children:

> are encouraged to participate fully, regardless of **disabilities** or medical needs.

Children with disabilities

Some children in our school have disabilities and consequently need additional resources. The school is committed to providing an environment that allows these children full access to all areas of learning. All our classroom entrances are wide enough for wheelchair access and the designated points of entry for our school also allow wheelchair access.

Teachers modify teaching and learning as appropriate for these children. For example, they may give additional time to children with disabilities to complete certain activities. In their planning, teachers ensure that they give children with disabilities the **opportunity** to develop skills in practical aspects of the curriculum.

Teachers ensure that the work of these children:

> takes account of their pace of learning and the equipment they use;

> takes account of the effort and concentration needed in oral work, or when using, for example, visual aids;

> is adapted or offers alternative activities in those subjects where children are able to manipulate tools or equipment, or use certain types of materials;

> allows **opportunities** for them to take part in educational visits and other activities linked to their studies;

> includes approaches that allow children with hearing impairments to learn about sound in science and music, and children with visual impairments to learn about light in science, and to use visual resources and images both in art and design and in design and technology; and

> uses assessment techniques that reflect their individual needs and abilities.

Summary/conclusion

This chapter examined dilemmas relating to equality, equality of opportunity and discrimination. Schools have to present policies on their approach to equal opportunities and demonstrate that they do not discriminate unfairly. But, given the problems relating to equality, and given very loose definitions of discrimination that are sometimes adopted, it is not as easy as it might first appear for schools to develop policies and practices that are coherent and credible.

With reference to pupils with SEN, the clearest policies are seeking to explain unequal (preferential) treatment of these pupils so that their opportunities to benefit from education are made more equal to those of pupils without SEN. This is expressed in terms of offering better opportunities through providing extra funding and support.

Funding through School Clusters: Self-interest and Co-operativeness

INTRODUCTION

Anyone diminishing the importance of money may be suspected of striking a pose, making Tom Stoppard's candour on completing Rosencranz and Guildenstern are Dead all the more refreshing. On being asked what the play was about, he replied 'It's about to make me very rich'.

School funding is certainly important, and this chapter explores an example – funding through school clusters (the LEA allocating money to schools so that the schools and others determine how it is to be equitably distributed). The development of approaches to SEN funding using school clusters involves balancing various responsibilities and interests of schools, the LEA, parents and others. One way of interpreting this is in terms of the degree of self-interest or co-operativeness required or demonstrated by the parties involved. I maintain that self-interest can be positioned somewhere between selfishness and self-negation. Co-operativeness is defined in relation to sociability and partnership.

It is suggested that self-interest could explain some parents, schools, lobby groups and others maximising resources for their own children considered to have SEN in a redistributive society without sufficient regard to the fair and equitable distribution of resources for others. Such self-interest may attract even greater funding (and is harder for the LEA to control) where one is dealing with 'non-normative' SEN such as dyslexia which is difficult to define.

Factors that can encourage co-operation include: the development of locally agreed criteria that seek to clarify how SEN is to be understood; the conviction and trust that provision for SEN can be made without the issuing of a statement of SEN; and the moderation of funding decisions.

Approaches such as the distribution of money to schools through school clusters may reflect a view that co-operativeness overrides self-interest. However, such an approach could equally be interpreted as assuming essential self-interest and circumventing or harnessing it.

A case study examines LEA funding and school clusters.

LEA funding and school clusters

LEA funding to schools has been the subject of intense debate. Guidance in *The Distribution of Resources to Support Inclusion* (Department for Education and Skills 2001c) included a recommended approach to financing in relation to: basic funding for all pupils; additional educational needs factors; cluster funding; support services; special school funding; and accountability.

With regard to school clusters, the funding approach relates to pupils who will often have complex learning and behaviour difficulties. It involves the LEA allocating resources for those pupils to a group of schools and LEA officers. The group then distributes 'additional' resources according to agreed criteria to supplement the resources already made available. A moderation system is used which may involve SEN co-ordinators. Proxy indicators are sometimes used to allocate funds for pupils with SEN whose needs are not complex. The model does not require pupils to have statements of SEN in order to be able to attract resources.

Self-interest and co-operation

Underpinning approaches that seek to ensure the equitable distribution of resources, even if they are not set out explicitly, are assumptions about the possible motives and probable behaviour of the participants in the process. Among these assumptions are ones relating to the degree of self-interest and the extent of co-operation that might be demonstrated.

This section therefore considers self-interest (comparing and contrasting it with self-ishness and self-negation) and co-operation (comparing and contrasting it with sociability and partnership).

Selfishness, self-interest and self-negation

Selfishness may be understood as acting with disregard for others. Self-negation, by contrast, implies acting in a way that puts the interests of others paramount, in an extreme example by risking one's life to save that of others. If these two concepts are taken to be opposite poles, somewhere between them lies self-interested behaviour.

If self-interest is understood as acting in a way that maximises benefits to oneself, it does not necessarily equate with selfishness. A person's interpretation of self-interest may include acting in a way that benefits members of his family and close friends. This may be criticised as doing no more than caring for people who, it is expected, would reciprocate. But if the moral obligations in society are interpreted in terms of some version of social contract theory, then most of a person's social actions could be understood as an exchange of services and of reciprocal relationships. Such an arrangement may, at its worst, reflect a limited and materialistic view of humanity. But it could not be considered entirely selfish.

Sociability, co-operation and partnership

Sociability can be regarded as an inclination to seek out social rather than solitary situations. Also, it can indicate a tendency to see situations more in terms of social implications rather than in predominantly personal and individualistic ways.

Related to sociability is the concept of co-operation seen as a form of enacting a social contract in both economic and moral terms. There is perhaps an implication that where people co-operate, the balance of power between them is ambiguous or shifting. If this is so, no one party can rest assured that they will be in a dominant position or a subservient position for very long. Consequently they are likely to regard co-operation as a necessary, effective and a safe middle way that will see them through the ups and downs of changing relationships.

However, co-operation understood in this way can be seen as a mirror image of the way that self-interest can be interpreted. Co-operation may be seen as behaviour likely to attract or require social responses from others. These responses, paradoxically, would be in the self-interest of the person behaving co-operatively. Such a relationship may be formalised by a structure such as the parent partnership service.

Partnership – for example the partnership between parents and schools – could be regarded as a mutually beneficial relationship, perhaps with the implication that the balance of power between the respective parties is about equal and likely to remain so for the foreseeable future.

Having examined both self-interest and co-operation it is now necessary to look at how each relates to special education.

Self-interest in special education

Maximising resources for SEN in a redistributive society

The actions of some parents, some schools and many lobby groups can be interpreted as self-interestedly seeking to maximise resources for particular children with SEN in the belief that they were, in this way, meeting their responsibilities. With parents, it is likely to be their own child. In the case of a school, it is likely to be the children in that particular school. For lobby groups, it is often a particular group of children with a certain 'type' of SEN, such as autistic spectrum disorder, dyslexia, dyspraxia and so on. While such self-interest requires co-operation, it is confined to a closely defined group having similar aims and values rather than with the wider community. If it is accurate to regard the actions of some of these participants as maximising resources for their 'own' children, then the consideration of other children is, understandably, not likely to be their highest priority.

Non-normative SEN

In the earlier chapter, 'Defining SEN: distinguishing goal-directed need and unconditional need', normative and non-normative conditions were briefly mentioned. Issues relating to non-normative conditions are further discussed below.

The expansion of SEN, especially of the non-normative SEN such as dyslexia, dyspraxia and autistic spectrum disorder, can be suspected as being as much related to self-interest as to addressing 'real' learning difficulties and disabilities. Such self-interest may be that of professionals, parents and related lobby groups. There is the potential for non-normative conditions to be defined in a way that could attract resources that would not be considered equitable in relation to the definition of SEN. The definition and identification of dyslexia may be taken as an example.

A report by the British Psychological Society (1999) provides a working definition of dyslexia as evident when 'accurate and fluent word reading and/or spelling develops very incompletely or with great difficulty' (ibid.: summary, paragraph 2). The definition requires that three aspects are evaluated through assessment:

1. Assessment considers whether the pupil is learning or has learnt accurate and fluent word reading and/or spelling very incompletely;

2. An evaluation is made of whether appropriate learning opportunities have been provided;

3. An assessment is carried out as to whether progress has been made only because of much additional effort and instruction and that the difficulties still persist (ibid.: summary, paragraph 7).

The report seeks to separate the identification of dyslexia from the assessment of SEN. While the identification of dyslexia draws on cognitive research and theory, SEN is seen as defined in relation to special educational provision. This allows for variation in the manifestation of SEN because what provision is deemed special may vary between LEAs, schools and teachers. The report intimates that local policy largely determines cut-off points for the provision of special education with reference to the continuum of what are considered mild, moderate or severe levels of dyslexia. The report considers that its working definition could be a starting point for social policy decisions. Features of the definition, especially severity and persistence, might, taken with other indicators, inform judgements by an LEA about severe and long-term SEN (ibid.: summary, paragraph 10).

But the working definition seems to leave room for inequity as it defines dyslexia as evident when 'accurate and fluent word reading and/or spelling develops very incompletely or with great difficulty' (ibid.: summary, paragraph 2). The expression 'with great difficulty' could be taken to imply that a child may be considered to have dyslexia if he could read at the same level as other children of the same age but that it had been difficult.

Similarly, the *Special Educational Needs Code of Practice* (Department for Education and Skills 2001b) does not offer a definition of dyslexia that would aid agreement about its identification. In considering the statutory assessment of SEN, the Code refers to evidence of attainment and progress, but also mentions '*expectations* of the child's performance' (ibid.: 7.39, italics added).

This seems to allow the (surely inequitable) statutory assessment of a child who reads at national age-average level to be considered as having SEN. This would be because he was judged to be behind expectations of his performance, for example based on evidence of his very high performance in other areas of the curriculum. This would presumably not occur with regard to a child who was average in all curriculum areas because his average reading would not be 'behind' other areas. Therefore a child who is only average in all curriculum subjects would not receive (rightly) a statutory assessment. At the same time, a child who is attaining at the same level in reading and who is above average in many areas of the curriculum might receive a statutory assessment that might in turn lead to a funded statement of SEN.

Where there is variation in what constitutes dyslexia, and at what level of significance reading, writing and spelling difficulties constitute an SEN, some parents may seek to argue for support and funding for their own child with no reference to the fairness to others. Indeed, it has been observed that it is 'an unhappy situation which allows the more vocal parents to achieve resources which may be equally needed by other pupils' (Hornby *et al.* 1997: 48). Where this is linked to loose definitions of what constitutes SEN, and an unchallenged predisposition to (over-) identify and classify apparent learning difficulties and disabilities on the part of some professionals, there is likely to be an over-expansion of SEN.

Non-normative SEN is an area in which it is particularly important to ensure that self-interest on the part of some parents, schools and lobby groups does not lead to inequity. In this context, some LEAs have developed local criteria for determining whether a statement in respect of specific learning difficulties should be used. In most cases this is based on a disparity between the pupils' chronological age and their reading age, usually of two years or more.

Such a definition might also try to take account of the issue of fluent reading and spelling developing 'with great difficulty', as the British Psychological Society (1999) definition has it. This could be done in the case of a child considered to have dyslexia by assessing the child's reading and spelling performance under timed conditions and comparing the outcome with that of children performing at age-average levels. It may be found that, in the time designated, the performance of the child thought to have dyslexia was, to a specified degree, behind that of the average child of the same age. If so, then this could be taken as evidence of difficulty with reading and spelling that could constitute a learning difficulty that might call for special educational provision to be made.

Co-operation in special education

Some aspects of SEN organisation and provision tend to encourage co-operation, examples being:

- locally agreed criteria aimed at clarifying how SEN and different types of SEN are to be understood;

- the conviction and trust that provision for SEN can be made without a statement of SEN being issued; and

- the moderation of funding decisions.

Locally agreed criteria

One strategy of encouraging co-operativeness in special education is to seek to demonstrate that a proposed system is fair and equitable, or at least *can* act fairly and equitably. Consider a parent who is requesting an LEA to carry out a statutory assessment of SEN that the LEA considers is unjustified. The negative response of an LEA that appears arbitrary is likely to be unfavourably regarded by the parent. However, another LEA may have worked over the years to reach a local agreement of what is considered to be the level of SEN warranting a statutory assessment, including developing criteria so far as possible to aid the process. A parent in the second LEA is unlikely to be pleased with the rejection of a request for statutory assessment. But where it can be demonstrated that the child does not meet the criteria (agreed by LEA officers, parents, schools and others) considered as indicating an SEN, it is more likely that the impartiality of the system will be recognised.

An important aspect of such an approach, if it is to be credible to parents and others, is that the funding for SEN should be as transparent as human ingenuity can devise. The issue is not one of getting more money for SEN but one of (whatever funds are allocated to pupils with SEN) ensuring that it is shared equitably. Even if an extra billion pounds were suddenly found for SEN, the issue of equitable distribution would remain and there would still be children that would justifiably be considered to have SEN and others that would not.

A difficulty, however, is that there is no unequivocal guidance from government about what SEN might mean. Such guidance as there is tends to be open to different interpretation being based on a contextual legal definition of SEN. Therefore, different LEAs may produce different notions of what they take SEN to be. There are two aspects to this.

First, an LEA may claim that its refusal to agree to a statutory assessment is a reflection of different levels of delegation. The LEA may consider that its schools already have funding to provide for certain levels of SEN, let us say pupils with moderate learning difficulties. Consequently, an LEA may refuse to carry out a statutory assessment because it claims that the schools in their area already have funds intended to provide for this type of SEN. In this case, the LEA has to demonstrate to schools and parents that this allocation of funding was agreed to cover pupils with moderate learning difficulties.

Also, an LEA may refuse to carry out a statutory assessment because a particular child does not 'have' SEN (e.g. dyslexia or severe learning difficulties) as defined in the LEA by agreement with local parents, officers and schools. Clear definitions of what constitutes SEN and different types of SEN are necessary before any meaningful discussion can take place about levels of delegation because levels of delegation can only be disputed if there is agreement that the child does 'have' a particular SEN.

Where LEAs can agree with other LEAs on common definitions, then it is more likely to seem reasonable to parents and others that this is a credible position to take regarding what SEN is. Similarly, the more that LEAs can agree to similar levels of delegation, the greater will be the consistency of their approach in relation to other LEAs and the greater the credibility of their position with parents and others. Attempts are being made to move towards more widely agreed approaches, for example by some LEAs within the London SEN Partnerships region.

Conviction that the provision for SEN would be made without a statement

When issuing and maintaining a statement of SEN, an LEA has to pay, in terms of money and staff time, for the bureaucracy that is normally in place to support this protection. This includes the cost of:

- writing reports for statutory assessment by educational psychologist, social worker, doctor, head teacher/teacher;

- time devoted by the special needs officer to progress and collate the statutory assessment within the specified time frame;

- time for a panel (or other mechanism) to determine whether the statutory assessment should lead to a statement;

- special needs officer time for drafting and agreeing a statement; and

- staff time spent on monitoring the provision specified on the statement through annual reviews and other means.

This leads to the question of whether a parent would be convinced that certain provision would be made without any statement at all. This would avoid most of the cost of the bureaucracy of the statement but still imply the cost of the provision itself. If no special provision is made, in the sense of something different from or additional to the ordinary, there is no point or justification in identifying the child as having SEN in the first place.

The moderation of funding decisions

The moderation of funding decisions is an aspect of an approach recommended in the document *The Distribution of Resources to Support Inclusion* (Department for Education and Skills 2001c). With regard to pupils with complex SEN, cluster funding is recommended. Where these SEN arise in a predictable way, LEAs may be able to enter into service-level agreements with certain schools to provide resources to them on a recurrent basis for providing specialist teaching and support (ibid.: section 8, section 4, sub-section 2). Where this is not possible, it may be helpful to allocate some resources to 'clusters' of schools. It is suggested that head teachers from such school clusters, together with the LEA, should agree on how the shared additional resources should be deployed to supplement those that are already available.

Moderation is suggested for requests for additional resources. This should be undertaken by 'peers' to help ensure transparency and that resources are fairly allocated among schools (ibid.: 8.4.3).

Cluster funding and co-operation

Towards the end of the previous section, cluster funding was mentioned. It will be seen that cluster funding involves an LEA delegating funding for SEN (that would otherwise be kept centrally) to 'clusters' of schools so that this can be distributed as schools and others think fair. This may be seen as an attempt to manage rational self-interest through encouraging co-operation in a particular sphere and over specified matters.

It will be remembered that the funding approach, related to pupils who will often have complex learning and behaviour difficulties, involves the LEA allocating resources for those pupils to a group of schools and LEA officers. The shifting power balance between these parties (including those between primary and secondary schools, those between the different schools within each phase and those between the LEA and the schools), is an incentive to co-operation.

The group then distributes additional resources according to agreed *criteria* to supplement the resources already made available. The importance of such criteria has been illustrated both in the present chapter and in the chapter 'Defining SEN: distinguishing goal-directed need and unconditional need'.

A *moderation* system is used which may involve SEN co-ordinators. This is a further mechanism for reassuring the parties that impartiality and equity are the aims.

The model does *not require pupils to have statements* of SEN in order to be able to attract resources. An added feature of this approach could be that (within legal parameters), should the number of statements in an LEA area increase, the funding for each will be proportionately decreased. This would be intended to reduce the incentives for (over-) identifying pupils thought to have SEN.

This approach is sometimes viewed with suspicion by some schools who may feel that they are left to make the hard decisions that LEA officers should be making and that the LEA are 'playing both ends against the middle'. Several factors can help such a system to work effectively.

First, all could be encouraged to view the LEA not as LEA officers and local politicians but as a corporate entity of which schools are a part. Naturally, in this organisation there would be some shared responsibilities and some distinct responsibilities. But there would be no distinction between 'LEA' and schools; schools would *be* the LEA as much as other participants. Secondly, the LEA finances should be transparent so that schools can see that the money they are involved in allocating is genuinely that which the LEA officers would have previously allocated and shared out. Thirdly, the tensions involved in allocating funds should act as a reality check for any school that ever thought that money always comes from 'them'. Finally, where schools have ever encouraged parents to seek statements of SEN to attract more funding, sharing responsibility for this, and seeing the consequences for other schools by having to see the overall system, may encourage the school to think more carefully.

Case study: Funding through school clusters

In the Education Bradford area, the funding involves 'mainstream support groups' (MSG). The process is being reviewed in the light of a wider review of additional educational needs funding and SEN funding. The description below outlines the situation before the review was completed.

The majority of children with SEN will have their needs met by their school using the 'age weighted pupil unit' and additional educational need funds in their budgets. A small number of children have exceptional needs which schools cannot meet from their own resources alone without some extra help from Education Bradford support services or from elsewhere beyond the school.

Schools are able to obtain additional resources from the MSG for these purposes. The resources the school will seek from the MSG will be additional to those already in the school which will continue to be used to meet pupils' SEN at the 'School Action' and 'School Action Plus' aspects of the graduated response.

The MSG in the Education Bradford area that consider requests for these additional resources from schools comprise local groups of professionals chaired by Achievement Support Managers. The MSG includes a Special Educational Needs Co-ordinator (SENCO) from each local group (or family) of schools. Representatives from the Multi Professional Team are also part of the MSG and include representatives from the Educational Psychology Service, the Learning Support Service and the School Improvement Officer. Some outreach support staff from special schools may also attend.

MSGs have a fixed amount of resources available to them to allocate to schools. Schools make their proposals for resources on a standard form and the MSG then consider all requests from their local area before allocating resources for pupils in the area according to the pupils' SEN. MSG funding may be used as a resource for a particular pupil or a number of pupils together.

The allocation to the school may be in the form of money to provide some time from a Special Needs Teaching Assistant, or in the form of time from the support services, such as specialist teachers or psychologists. It is then the school's responsibility to arrange the support that the pupils need. Education Bradford monitors the school's use of these resources.

The MSG meets once a year to consider the proposals made by schools in the area and to allocate resources to the schools. Usually, the meeting, held in the summer term, makes an allocation of resources for the whole of the following year so that the school can plan programmes better.

Where a group of schools within a family (a local cluster of primary and secondary schools) makes a joint proposal to meet the SEN of their pupils, the area MSG can allocate resources to the group of schools as a whole. The school group then has the responsibility and flexibility to use the resources for the planned purpose and to report back to the MSG. Education Bradford continues to monitor the use of these resources by the schools concerned.

Education Bradford regularly monitors decisions made by the MSG to make sure that decisions are made consistently by the MSG across Bradford.

(Based on information kindly provided by Education Bradford)

Summary/conclusion

This chapter maintains that the development of approaches to SEN funding using school clusters involves balancing various responsibilities and interests of schools, the LEA, parents and others. This was interpreted in terms of the degree of self-interest or co-operativeness of the parties involved. Self-interest was one explanation of how parents, schools, lobby groups and others maximise resources for their own children considered to have SEN in a redistributive society without sufficient regard to the fair and equitable distribution of resources for others. Such self-interest tends to be more difficult to reconcile with the interests of others when one is dealing with 'non-normative' types of SEN, such as dyslexia, which are difficult to define. Attempts to encourage co-operation were considered: locally agreed criteria; the conviction that provision for SEN can be made without the issuing of a statement of SEN; and the moderation of funding decisions. While funding through school clusters may reflect a view that co-operativeness overrides self-interest, this may be too idealistic. It would be more realistic to think in terms of checks and balances, with participants accepting that to advance their own interests they also have to take into account those of others.

5

Parents, LEA and SENDIST: Balance of Power

INTRODUCTION

Power, and those possessing it, is often treated with suspicion, if not scorn, as when Aldous Huxley stated that so long as men worship the Caesars and Napoleons, Caesars and Napoleons will duly rise and make them miserable. Even the more modest power of those who make decisions concerning special education may be viewed circumspectly.

In this chapter, I consider the relationship between politics, power and resources. I explain the nature of decision-making power and then consider the notion in relation to SEN, focusing on the power to identify pupils at Early Years Action/School Action, Early Years Action Plus/School Action Plus, and in relation to statutory assessment.

Mention is made of guidance on preventing and resolving disagreements between parents and local education authorities concerning SEN. Turning to a consideration of the Special Educational Needs and Disability Tribunal (SENDIST) the chapter outlines the role of the Tribunal. It then looks at the appeals to the SENDIST in terms of the power of parent lobby groups and of tensions between LEA powers and those of the SENDIST.

In a case study, the parent of a child with autism gives her account of the process of getting a statement for her child and of appealing to the SEN Tribunal.

Parents, the LEA and the SENDIST

Parents sometimes report the difficulties they have had getting their child's SEN recognised and provided for to their satisfaction. In recently published research into whether current legislation is protecting the interests of disabled children in residential schools, almost all the parents interviewed felt they had to 'fight' the local authority to get 'their child's needs met' (Morris *et al.* 2003: 72). In a recent SENCO forum maintained by the

British Educational Technology and Communications Agency, the case for labelling children with SEN as a way of obtaining resources and help was made by four forum members who, regarding their children, 'had struggled to have their needs met' (Wedell 2003: 107).

Underlying such accounts may be different perspectives of when and if a statement is necessary for a particular child and what constitutes appropriate provision.

Further considerations include the power of the school to identify SEN, the power of the LEA to choose whether or not to carry out a statutory assessment or issue a statement of SEN and the power of parents and others in demanding a statement. Also important is the role of the SEN and Disability Tribunal in appeals concerning the issuing of statements and other matters.

Politics, power and resources

One view of politics relates it to 'the production, distribution and use of resources in the course of social existence' (Haywood 1999: 58). While the so-called 'needs' and wants of members of society are without bounds, resources are necessarily finite. Politics may therefore be regarded as the debate, negotiation and power struggle permeating the distribution of resources. To the extent that politics is involved in the allocation of scarce resources (Haywood 1999: 63), the political process may be considered on three different levels. At the personal and family level, it is manifested in regular face-to-face contact (deciding how time and money is spent). At the tier of the community, it involves local and regional representative government as well as the workplace and public institutions. At the national level, it concerns national government, political parties and pressure groups.

Decision-making power

In a classic study, *A Critique of the Ruling Elite Model*, Dahl (1958) maintained that any view of the United States of America that proposed that it was ruled by a permanent, identifiable ruling elite was unfounded. He maintained that before any claim that there was a ruling elite could be justifiably made, three criteria must be met:

1. the proposed ruling elite must be a clearly defined group;

2. several important political decisions must be identified in which the preferences of the ruling elite oppose those of other groups; and

3. evidence must be presented to demonstrate that the preferences of the elite have regularly prevailed over those of other groups.

Underlying this analysis is the implication that power concerns being able to influence or even determine the decision-making process (decision-making power).

Dahl's later (1963) study in New Hampshire concentrated on the local community and considered public education (and also urban renewal and nominating political candidates). The study indicated that local citizens exerted much less power and influence than those having economic power and political privilege. While this demonstrated the existence of a decision-making 'elite', the study found that the elite was different in the different areas of study. The people constituting the elite influencing education were not the elite exerting power in urban renewal or in nominating political candidates. This suggested that there is no one permanent ruling elite but many elites exerting power in different fields.

For anyone trying unsuccessfully to influence education including special education as a so-called ordinary citizen, the possibility that there may be a distinction between a permanent ruling elite and a more localised elite that tends to get its own way may offer rather cold comfort. Whether or not the elite that dominates special education does or does not monopolise other areas of social life is by the way. An important question is therefore, 'Is there evidence of the existence of one elite or several elites that influence special education in a way that may not reflect what the majority might want?'.

Decision-making power and special education

The aspect of decision-making power to be considered in this section is the fundamental power of deciding who has SEN both in terms of judgements made in a setting or school and in terms of LEA-initiated statutory assessment and statements of SEN for children of compulsory school age. This power involves the allocation (in fact the reallocation) of resources to some children and some schools over others. The resources may be in the form of funds that the school can convert into support such as staff or equipment. Or they may be in the form of staff employed by the LEA which in turn, of course, the LEA has to pay for.

Early Years Action/School Action and Early Years Action Plus/School Action Plus

Under the *Special Educational Needs Code of Practice* (DfES 2001b), the school or setting that a child attends normally decides whether a child is to be considered to have SEN at the level of Early Years Action/School Action. In Early Years Action, an early years practitioner (working day to day with the child) or the SENCO identifies that the child has SEN. Together they provide interventions different from or additional to those normally provided as part of the setting's usual 'curriculum offer and strategies' (ibid.: chapter 4, section 20).

At School Action, a class or subject teacher identifies that a pupil has SEN and provides interventions additional to or different from those provided as part of 'the school's usual differentiated curriculum offer and strategies' (ibid.: 5.43, 6.50).

The school or setting decides in consultation with parents whether intervention is necessary at Early Years Action Plus or School Action Plus. At Early Years Action Plus, an early years practitioner, working day to day with the child, and the SENCO are given advice or support from outside specialists (ibid.: 4.29). At School Action Plus, a class or subject teacher and the SENCO are given advice or support from outside specialists (ibid.: 5.54, 6.62).

The Code states that, in the early years, 'Once practitioners have identified that the child has special educational needs, the setting should intervene through Early Years Action' (ibid.: 4.11). The setting is expected to 'judge how to tell the parents that their child is receiving special educational provision because their child has SEN' (ibid.: 4.12). Regarding Early Years Action Plus, which 'is characterised by the involvement of external support services' (ibid.: 4.29), consultation with parents is expected. The Code advises that 'A request for help from external services is likely to follow a decision by the SENCO and colleagues, in consultation with parents, at a meeting to review the child's IEP' (ibid.: 4.30).

In the primary phase it is the class teacher or the SENCO that has the power to identify whether or not a child is considered to have SEN. The Code asserts, 'When a class teacher or SENCO identifies a child with SEN the class teacher should provide interventions that are <u>additional to</u> or <u>different from</u> those provided as part of the school's usual differentiated curriculum offer and strategies (*School Action*)' (ibid.: 5.34). Regarding School Action Plus, 'A request for help from external services is likely to follow a decision taken by the SENCO and colleagues, in consultation with parents, at a meeting to review the child's IEP' (ibid.: 5.54).

In the secondary sector, the identification of a pupil requiring 'School Action' intervention is made by 'a subject teacher, member of the pastoral team or SENCO' (ibid.: 6.50). At School Action Plus, 'A request for external help is likely to follow a decision taken by the SENCO and colleagues, in consultation with parents, at a meeting to review the child's IEP' (ibid.: 6.62).

Statutory assessment

There are three paths for referral to an LEA for statutory assessment. The first route is a request for such an assessment by a school or setting. In the early years, 'Parents, schools and settings can make a request to the LEA for a statutory assessment ... The LEA is then responsible for determining whether a statutory assessment is required' (ibid.: 4.34). At the primary phase, a request may be made 'by a school to an LEA' (ibid.: 5.62). In the secondary sector, help given at School Action Plus may be insufficient to enable the pupil to make adequate progress. If so, 'It will then be necessary for the school, in consultation with the parents and any statutory agency already involved, to consider whether to ask the LEA to initiate a statutory assessment' (ibid.: 6.70). This is summarised in the Education Act 1996, section 329A, which requires that schools and relevant nursery education providers have a statutory right to ask the LEA to conduct a statutory assessment or reassessment of a child's special educational needs (see Code 7.9).

The second referral path is a request for assessment from a parent (ibid.: 7.21–29), while the third route is through a request from an agency such as a health authority or social services department (ibid.: 7.15).

Whether the route for referral is a school or setting, or a parent or another agency, the decision-making power is with the LEA. However, in many cases, part of the decision-making process is reached only after decisions have been made much earlier by the school or setting (Early Years Action/School Action) or by the school or setting in consultation with parents and other agencies (Early Years Action Plus/School Action Plus). Although it is possible for a statement to be issued for a child without the child having been identified at Early Years Action/Action Plus or School Action/Action Plus, this is unusual.

Preventing and resolving disagreements

Under the Education Act 1996, section 322B, a local authority must make arrangements that include the appointment of independent persons with a view to avoiding or resolving disagreements between:

- authorities; and
- parents of children in their area

concerning the way LEAs and maintained schools carry out their responsibilities toward children with SEN. Also, a local authority has to make arrangements 'with a view to' avoiding or resolving disagreements between parents and certain schools about the SEN provision made for their child.

Informal disagreement resolution agreements are intended to stop long-term problems developing and reducing in time the number of disputes going to the Special Educational Needs and Disability Tribunal (see also Department for Education and Skills 2001b, chapter 2, section 22–30). Among approaches used are parent partnerships and mediation services.

The role of the Special Educational Needs and Disability Tribunal (SENDIST)

The SENDIST, an independent tribunal originally set up by an Act of Parliament of 1993 as the SEN Tribunal, seeks to resolve disputes between parents and an LEA. Its remit was widened in 2001 to take account of the requirements of the Special Educational Needs and Disability Rights in Education Act 2001 (Department for Education and Employment, Scottish Executive, Scotland Office, Cynulliad Cenedlaethol Cymru 2001). The SENDIST considers parents' appeals against the decisions of an LEA about a child's SEN when the parents and the LEA cannot reach agreement. The Tribunal, whose decisions are final, has jurisdiction over LEAs but not over individual schools.

Parents can appeal to SENDIST if the LEA:

- refuses to carry out a formal assessment of SEN on their child; or
- refuses to issue a statement of the child's SEN.

If the LEA has made a statement, or if they have changed an earlier statement, parents may appeal against:

- the parts of the statement describing the child's SEN (part 2);
- the parts which set out the special educational help that the LEA considers the child should receive (part 3);
- the school named in the statement (part 4); or
- the LEA not naming a school.

Parents may appeal if the LEA:

- refuses to change the school named in the child's statement where the statement is at least one year old;
- refuses to reassess the child's SEN if the LEA has not made a new assessment for at least six months;
- decides not to maintain the child's statement;
- decides not to change the statement; or
- has discriminated against a child unfairly because of the child's disability.

Every year since the SEN Tribunal was formed (and since it became the SENDIST), there has been an increase in appeals registered. By the year 2001–2 it registered 3,048 appeals, compared with 1,161 in 1994–5 (Special Educational Needs Tribunal 2002: 5–6). The categories for most appeals in the year 2001–2 were as follows:

- refusal to assess (37.4%);
- the contents of a statement parts 2, 3 and 4 (24.0%);

- the contents of the statement parts 2 and 3 (13.3%);

- the contents of the statement part 4 (11.2%);

- refusal to make a statement (8.0%).

(ibid. 2002: 7)

Appeals to the SENDIST: the power of parent lobby groups?

The outcomes of appeals to the SENDIST indicate that they are usually successful from the point of view of parents, with 76 per cent of appeals succeeding in 2001–2. In all types of appeal, except those against 'refusal to reassess' and 'refusal to make a statement', the percentage of appeals upheld was 67 per cent or above. In one area (appeals against the contents of a statement parts 2, 3 and 4) it was 93 per cent. Given this tendency for parents to be successful in appeals it is informative to consider the types of SEN that are the subject of appeals.

The main types of SEN of pupils whose cases were registered with the SENDIST in the year 2000–1 were:

- literacy, including specific learning difficulties (34.5%);

- autism (16.1%);

- emotional and behavioural difficulties (14.2%); and

- speech and language difficulties (10.2%).

(Special Educational Needs Tribunal 2002: 8)

Almost 77 per cent of appeals were related to these four areas while the remaining appeals concerned physical disabilities, moderate learning difficulties, severe learning difficulties, hearing impairment, epilepsy, visual impairment, multisensory impairment and 'other/unknown' SEN.

As long ago as the first year of the Tribunal's operation, analyses of the Tribunal cases showed that the majority of the appeals were for dyslexia. It appeared that LEAs were having to pay for expensive provision for a number of children considered to have dyslexia, affecting their spending on other areas of SEN provision (House of Commons 1995). Subsequently, as the remit of autism was widened to comprise 'autistic spectrum disorder', there has been an increase in such cases referred to the Tribunal.

It is not possible for the Tribunal in its annual report to relate the percentages concerning particular areas of SEN (e.g. specific learning difficulties, autism) with the percentages of areas of SEN as they appear to exist nationally. National level data is unavailable at present. However, when such data become available, if the Tribunal were to employ it, this would make it possible to see, for example, whether any areas of SEN appeared to be of a greater or lesser proportion than the national prevalence.

Discrepancies might suggest the need to consider possible reasons for the under- or over-representation of certain forms of SEN in appeals.

If there were such apparent under- or over-representation, one possible influence could be the differential power of lobby groups. But given the present dearth of information, it is not clear whether appeals to the SENDIST according to particular types of SEN reflect the differential power of particular lobby groups purporting to represent the interests of children with these conditions or whether other factors are responsible.

Quite early in the development of the Tribunal, concerns were expressed that articulate parents would dominate the system (Fish and Evans 1995; Bibby and Lunt 1996). Annual reports of the SENDIST do not at present provide information on the social background of the parents who appealed, so it is not possible to see whether appeals are associated with parents of one social background or another. Some involved in education continue to express the view that earlier concerns about parents affecting the balance of funding have been subsequently supported (e.g. Evans and Gerber 2000).

Perhaps one should not expect parents to be greatly concerned with other children when it comes to seeking extra money to support their own child. Theirs is not the prime responsibility to see that all children get a fair share of SEN and other funding. That is the duty of the LEA and others. This, in turn, points to the importance of LEA-agreed approaches to the identification of pupils with SEN discussed in the earlier chapter, 'Defining SEN: distinguishing goal-directed needs and unconditional needs'.

Tensions between LEA approaches and SENDIST powers

The annual report of the Tribunal in the year 1999–2000 (Special Educational Needs Tribunal 2000) rejected the possibility of seeking consistency with regard to the main SEN of children. This was because the Tribunal is looking at individual cases rather than all at the same time, and the report emphasised that no two cases are the same. The document stated that: 'The difficulties, disabilities, experiences and circumstances of the children whose educational needs we consider vary almost infinitely. Direct comparisons between two apparently similar cases are nearly always misleading' (ibid.: 16). The Tribunal recognises the view that it might be considered desirable to link test results and certain levels of support but rejects this as 'mechanistic' and does not consider that the Tribunal should act consistently in that sense.

In contrast to this view, when LEAs consider broad funding issues and the cost of support for individual pupils, they often assume that there are broad differences. For example, a child with profound learning difficulties is assumed to require more support and funding that a child with moderate learning difficulties (see also Farrell 2004, chapter 3).

In the LEA context, assumptions are made about children considered together including the level of support likely to be suitable. Many LEAs and others are seeking to allocate support and funding consistently and according to some transparent system related to local criteria, agreed through consultation. Such an approach allows the fine-tuning of funding and support to be made from other funds that the school receives in relation to SEN generally.

Where local agreement does not complement individually based SENDIST decisions, and where these decisions relate to funding, SENDIST powers can have the effect of redistributing funds to pupils who, from a local perspective, have lower levels of 'need' than similar pupils who receive no extra support.

Case study: a parent's account

This case study presents a parent's view of getting her child's SEN recognised and supported by what the parent considers suitable provision. Mrs C.'s daughter, Anne, has autism and is the second of two children. (Names have been changed to retain confidentiality.)

'I am not sure when I became aware that there were problems with Anne. When she was a baby she cried much more than my previous child. She was ill much of the time with colds and coughs. By the time she was eight months old she had very strong preferences for only two foods – yoghurt and stewed apple – and would eat little else. She had started babbling, but this did not develop and she became more and more quiet.

'At 14 months I began to think something was wrong. Something seemed to be odd about her senses. An ambulance would pass making a terrific noise and she would show no sign of having heard anything. Yet she would turn to the slightest sound. Someone took a flash photograph and instead of covering her eyes she put her hands over her ears! Her equilibrium did not seem to be quite right because she would walk on a baby slope in the shape of a toy bridge and, in the middle, she would freeze as if she were dizzy. Yet she did not seem to have any fear on an equilibrium bar.

'At an 18 months developmental check the doctor thought she might be deaf because of her apparent lack of response to sounds. Around this time, I began to read about possible reasons why children's language and talking might not develop normally, and one of the possible explanations mentioned was that the child might be autistic. I then read a book about autism and some of the descriptions seemed to fit some of Anne's behaviours. For example, she did not point to things or seem to understand what pointing meant; she did not wave goodbye; she did not seem to miss me if I went away. There was no sociability, no connection. She just liked playing with bubbles and rattles.

'At 20 months I took her to see a paediatrician. I was anxious and uncomfortable and this seemed to convey itself to Anne who was overactive and unco-operative at the consultation. The paediatrician referred her to the Maudsley Hospital. There the doctor diagnosed classical autism.

'Through the Portage home-visiting service, which was helping Anne, I began to meet other parents whose children had autism. The Portage worker suggested that Anne might benefit from having a statement of SEN. When Anne was about three years old I contacted the National Autistic Society. Anne attended a special needs playgroup for one session per week and had Portage work once a week.

'She started mainstream nursery early in the summer term, before she was four. A speech and language therapist assessed Anne's language as being very delayed. I raised the question of a statement but this was not followed up. She had several auditory tests which I felt were a waste of time because I knew that there was nothing physically wrong with her hearing, only her odd responses to sounds. Anne had a one-to-one helper and, for two months, this seemed to work well.

'But over the summer holidays, the nursery underwent rebuilding work to extend it. When Anne returned in September there were more children, there was more noise and there was a bigger area, and she did not settle. She had problems with the social rules that were necessary in the nursery. For example, if the teacher was reading a story, she naturally expected the whole group to listen. Anne could not understand the language of the story and she would not listen. She used to cry a lot. This disrupted the other children because, when they saw Anne going off they would want to go off too. By October, it was clear that Anne was unhappy at the nursery and that the provision was not suiting her.

'I then decided to take her to a special nursery in a nearby town. This was an independent nursery for children with special educational needs in communication and behaviour and I paid for the place. The family moved house soon after so that Anne did not have to travel to her new nursery. When Anne reached the age of 5, the LEA had no school placement for her.

'Neither the LEA in our previous area nor the LEA in our new area had made a statement of SEN for Anne. When Anne was nearly 5, I had a meeting with an educational psychologist who wrote a report along with the special independent nursery supporting the need for a statement of SEN.

'In July of that year Anne received a statement, but the LEA had no suitable place, so part 4 of the statement, which specifies the placement, was left blank. Part 5 of the statement, which specified that Anne needed speech and language therapy, was entered as a non-educational need. Because there was no other place, the special independent nursery had Anne for an extra year, the reception year, and the LEA paid for the placement.

'Anne did not have an annual review when she was six years old. She transferred to a special school for autistic children. She was in a group of seven to eight children and she seemed to be making reasonable progress. Her first annual review, which took place when she was 7, seemed to confirm this.

'However, when Anne was eight years old she was placed in a different group and found this difficult, throwing tantrums and showing very resistant behaviour. Her progress slowed in both reading and number and her targets for the coming year seemed to me to be insufficiently ambitious. The school began to seem too rigid in its approach and seemed unable to offer flexibility in what she could participate in. For example, she hated horse-riding and there seemed to be no flexibility with this. I began to lose confidence in the school and took her out of school for two months. During this time, I noticed Anne was progressing much better. In September that year I decided not to send Anne back to school.

'I had heard of a programme called the Sonrise programme. Another parent of an autistic child was following this and asked me to help as a paid facilitator for her son. It involved long-term, intensive one-to-one work. It seemed to be benefiting her son whose eye contact and sociability seemed to be improving. I began to think that Anne might benefit from the programme.

'In the September that Anne was nine years old, I went to see a solicitor for advice about having her statement changed to provide funding for Anne to follow the programme at home. It emerged that part

4 of the statement still had the name of the nursery that Anne had attended when she was five years old as her present placement. So it looked as though there could be an opportunity to have the statement changed. The LEA refused to comply so I decided to appeal to the SEN Tribunal.

'By the time the appeal took place a year later, I had spent £5,000 on a barrister, a report from an educational psychologist and solicitor's fees. The appeal was unsuccessful.

'I kept Anne at home, following the programme, without any help as far as funding is concerned. I get some voluntary help from a parent who works with Anne as a facilitator. The school did not appear interested in the home programme. They offered a reintegration programme to help Anne return to school, but as this was not what the Tribunal had directed I declined it. I requested a meeting with officers at the LEA and the parent partnership representative but that did not take place until after I had written to the director of education asking for an annual review of Anne's statement. The meeting, in fact, achieved nothing.

'Every September an educational welfare officer visits me at home to enquire why Anne is not at school. Anne is now 13 years old.'

Summary/conclusion

This chapter considered the relationship between politics, power and resources. It examined decision-making power in relation to SEN with regard to the power to identify pupils at Early Years Action/School Action; Early Years Action Plus/School Action Plus; and in relation to statutory assessment. I considered appeals to the Special Educational Needs and Disability Tribunal (SENDIST) in terms of the power of parent lobby groups and of tensions between LEA powers and those of the SENDIST. An account of the parent of a child with autism illustrated the complexities of the different sources of power or lack of power (parent, LEA officers, lawyers, school, SENDIST) in the process of getting a statement and of appealing on another matter to the SEN Tribunal.

While there is much talk of partnership in special education, such an arrangement may depend on a close balance of power in order to work (as was suggested in the chapter 'Funding through school clusters: self-interest and co-operativeness'). Trust has the opportunity to develop where different parties perceive they can each fairly influence the outcomes. Where trust begins to break down, the sources of power and how they are balanced become even more important as they are all that the different parties can fall back on.

6

The Special Education Needs Forum: Representation

INTRODUCTION

'I don't like my music,' Frederick Lowe confessed, 'but what is my opinion against that of millions of others?' As far as diverse opinions are concerned, fora are recognised as one of the ways in which they can be brought together, recognised and possibly resolved. At the heart of fora is the principle of representation, that is an attempt to give voice to the views of those who are unable to participate directly.

Among the fora in education are regional and local ones that focus on SEN issues bringing together parents; officers for the education, health and social services; and others. Any SEN forum that seeks to hear and discuss differing views assumes that participants represent, in some way, others who cannot be present. In this chapter, therefore, representation is defined and some criticisms of representation in a capitalist liberal democracy are outlined. Different forms of representation are considered: choosing people with a good education and with wide experience; mandated representation; and characteristic representation.

I examine the influence of children's views and child advocacy, disability interest groups and parent groups in special education.

The chapter considers the Special Educational Needs Code of Practice (Department for Education and Skills 2001b) guidance, which seeks to include, in the identification of SEN and subsequent provision, the views of children, either directly or through advocacy.

I look at the particular role of disability groups as lobbyists. The chapter examines whether an unrelated person with, say, a physical disability can represent a child, for example with profound and multiple learning difficulties, simply because both can be apparently brought together under a broad conception of disability. Such narrow notions of representation are considered as a recipe for social division and conflict.

The role of parents is considered, including the extent to which parents can represent children with SEN.

A case study is presented describing the formation and operation of an 'SEN forum' for the parents and carers of children with SEN which has developed links with officers from the education, social and health services, and others. Representation can be problematic, but it is suggested that if potential and real difficulties and issues are addressed, attempts to develop consensus through dialogue by such means as SEN fora can be worthwhile.

The SEN forum: three questions

Any kind of forum assumes that it can tap into the views of a wider range of people than those attending meetings because in some way those present are representatives. The SEN forum is no exception. Questions arising are:

- Which groups have a legitimate interest in SEN and therefore a 'right' to represent interests of children with SEN?
- What weight should be placed on the respective views of participants?
- Where views differ, what is the mechanism for seeking to resolve differences?

When such matters are considered, the concept of representation and practicalities relating to it reveal themselves as far from straightforward. Towards the end of this chapter, the three questions will be revisited. First, it is necessary to consider some limitations of representation in general, some of its forms, and issues arising from the representation of children with SEN by the children themselves, advocates, disability groups and parents.

Representation and its limitations in a capitalist liberal democracy

Representation is an important element of a capitalist liberal democracy. It has been suggested that the attraction of a liberal democracy is 'its capacity to blend elite rule with a significant measure of popular participation' (Haywood 1999: 227). Professional politicians rule, but are placed in power by the electorate who can equally well vote them out in national elections. Accountability is not merely restricted to elections but is exerted though various interest groups and cause groups. This dispersal of political power leads to liberal democracies sometimes being described as 'pluralist democracies'.

Despite the potential benefits of representation, however limited, the elite element of such an arrangement has not escaped criticism. One view is that, while power is held by an elite, the fact that there are competing elites ensures that the popular voice is heard. But an alternative perspective (Mills 1956) is that industrial societies are dominated by a small, continuing and exclusive 'power elite' that controls the main hierarchies and organisations. Power is largely institutional and vested in non-elected bodies such as the police, the judiciary, the military and the bureaucracy (see also the chapter 'Parents, the LEA and the SENDIST: balance of power' for further comments on elites).

From another viewpoint, liberal democracy has been criticised for not involving sufficient popular participation (e.g. Bottomore 1993). Suggestions to improve this have included the harnessing of information and communications technology, more use of referenda, greater involvement of pressure groups and organisationally flatter and less bureaucratic political parties.

Forms of representation

The implication of representation in politics is that one person or a group of people 'stands for' a much wider group of others. Among the ways that representation can be understood are:

- choosing people with a good education and wide experience;
- mandated representatives; and
- characteristic representation.

Well-educated representatives with wide experience

Representatives are sometimes perceived as members of society who know better than others how to make political decisions. They may be assumed to know better because of their background or education or because of experience in the political sphere. According to this view, politicians should not be completely under the sway of those who have elected them but should (within the parameters of the political manifesto on which they stood for election) make up their own minds on issues.

Among the difficulties with this is that education and even experience, of itself, is no guarantee of good moral judgement. Also, to avoid the problem of the representative becoming increasingly detached from the electorate, it is often thought necessary that the delegate should interact frequently with those represented, for example in local open meetings. The extent to which this is practicable increases in proportion to the degree of responsibility that the delegate assumes. The greater the responsibility and the greater the need for consultation, the more difficult it is to find the time for direct personal contact with those one seeks to represent.

Mandated representatives

Another perspective is that politicians are in place because they were elected and mandated by the people to express the views of those people and to act as they would act were they present.

Such a view is complicated by the fact that large groups of people often differ in their views, if not on broad policy, then on interpretations of it and of how policy ends should be achieved. Additionally, election systems do not always represent views proportionately. A 'first past the post' system may leave the majority of the electorate feeling that they are not represented, even if everyone who was eligible to vote did so. The notion of a mandate cannot only act as an indication of what a particular political party proposes, but it can unduly constrain politicians if circumstances develop in an unexpected way. This can lead to the accusation of making a U-turn in terms of what was originally promised, even if taking a different view might be justified in the light of unexpected events.

Characteristic respresentation

Yet another position is that politicians should represent other members of society in the sense that they are like them in terms of social background, gender, ethnicity, disability and other characteristics. They should be a microcosm of society at large. This position is sometimes referred to as 'characteristic representation'.

If a 'top down' view of such representation is taken, it might imply a quota system of ensuring a certain number of representatives of each gender, different social backgrounds, different ethnic backgrounds and so on. An assumption is that only people who are from a particular group can adequately speak up for its interests. But to try to represent every view could become a statistical nightmare, for not only proportionate representations of different groups would be necessary, but also, presumably, combinations of these groups. For example, there would be a certain number of white, 'middle class' educated males, a certain number of white, 'working class' women, and a certain number of black, disabled teenagers, and so on. More fundamentally, it could be patronising to assume that broadly defined groups all have the same or even similar views. This might be considered less of a problem if the representative was chosen by those represented.

The views of children, disability lobby groups and parents in SEN

Among those who seek to represent the views of children are children themselves, or advocates for a particular child, disability lobby groups and parents.

The views of children and their representation

The *Special Educational Needs Code of Practice* (Department for Education and Skills 2001b) encourages the participation of pupils with SEN in making decisions and exercising choices about their education and other matters. With regard to involving pupils in assessment and decision-making it is suggested that schools and professionals may need to (among other things): 'draw upon the experience of any local pupil support or advocacy services for children which might offer additional advice or assistance' (ibid.: chapter 3, section 18).

Also, schools and education authorities 'should be aware of the wider range of participation and advocacy services for children and young people and their families being developed in partnership with health and social service departments' (ibid.: 3.20).

The implications of the Code are that, where it is possible, children should be directly involved in assessment and decision-making, and where this is not possible, pupils' views should be represented as far as they can be discerned.

At a more general level, as the Code notes, many schools have school councils 'or other mechanisms for including and representing all pupils in the organisation and management of the school' (ibid.: 3.13). Such participation does not include pupils' contributions to the development of policy concerning SEN. In this respect the representation of pupils is at a different level in some circumstances to that of others with an interest or stake in special education.

Disability interest groups

Interest groups may seem, at first sight, an example of desirable wider democratic participation. But the same difficulties attach to such groups as attach to characteristic representation generally.

One implication of disability interest groups is that it is only those who have disabilities who can truly know what the experience of disability is like. Therefore, it may be suggested, their views have a special value in representing other disabled people. Such a view is open to question even if disabled adults are purporting to represent other disabled adults. (Similar questions may be raised about the principle applied to all groups such as members of ethnic minorities or ethnic majorities, women, men, and so on.)

The first difficulty is that it is unjustifiable to simply assume that because someone is a member of a broadly defined group of 'disabled' people, his or her views are likely to be the same as other disabled people. If this assumption were correct, then should there not be differences within any group identified as disabled according to such groupings as: disabled women, disabled men, disabled members of a particular ethnic group, of a particular age or a particular social background? Any differences would presumably be subsumed under a single label of 'disability'.

A second challenge for disabled interest groups is that there are also differences of views among physically disabled adults about such matters as separate education in special schools. Some deaf people (not all) argue for separate special schools for deaf children where they can learn their 'own language'. Other disabled people argue for the closure of all special schools, seeing them as oppressive.

A third issue is that the definition of disability has been widened by so-called disability theorists to include groups that have huge differences. For example, a deaf-blind person with profound and multiple learning difficulties who requires lifelong care is brought together with a person of average intelligence or above who has a full-time professional job and perhaps a paralysed limb because they are both 'disabled'. (Similar all-embracing thinking in the USA groups together very able children with children who have profound learning difficulties, because they are both 'exceptional'.)

A fourth issue is that assuming that a member of a group has an exclusive or even a privileged insight into other members seems to be a very limited view of human capacities for mutual understanding. Only women can represent women, only men can represent men, only whites can represent whites, only blacks can represent blacks, only people with learning difficulties and disabilities can represent one another. Such views are likely to provide a recipe for social division and in-fighting that is counter-productive. How would such views respond in the numerous situations when it is necessary to take a non-factional overview? A weaker version of this view is that a woman is more likely to understand the position of another woman than a man is, and vice versa.

It is difficult to know or to decide which of a person's identities should be the defining one. Is a person's identity defined according to disability, gender, social class, personal interests, age, place of residence or one of a hundred other potential identifiers? What is the supposed shared 'experience' of people with such diverse identities, and what is meant by the term 'experience' in this context? Is reason really powerless to influence people, whatever they see as their identities?

If the above difficulties are relevant it would suggest that care be taken that there is no simplistic assumption that one disabled person can automatically speak for other disabled people. However, in a general sense, where a representative of such a group draws on personal experience and puts the case of others that have been brought to his attention the representative may make a valuable contribution to a forum.

Parents as representatives of their child's interests and those of other parents

To what extent can parents represent children with SEN? The *Special Educational Needs Code of Practice* (Department for Education and Skills 2001b) provides guidance which includes the representations of parents concerning the special education of their children. When parents receive a proposed statement of SEN from an LEA they: 'have a right to state a preference for the maintained school their child should attend and to make representations to, and hold meetings with, the LEA' (ibid.: chapter 8, section 57). 'Parents may express a preference for any maintained school they wish their child to attend, or make representations for a placement in any other school' (ibid.: 8.60).

Parental representations about a proposed statement of SEN include that:

> (a) they may within 15 days make representations to the LEA, and require that a meeting be arranged with an officer of the LEA to discuss the contents of the statement;
>
> (b) within 15 days of meeting the officer, the parents may make further representations or, if they disagree with any part of the assessment, require further meetings to be arranged with appropriate people within the LEA to discuss the advice given (ibid.: 8.105).

These 'representations' involve the parents expressing views that they believe reflect the interests of their child. In this sense they are representing the child. There are occasions, naturally, where the wishes of the child can be ascertained and where these conflict with the views of the parents. On other occasions, two parents may disagree about how best to proceed. How such matters are resolved (if they are resolved) varies from situation to situation. A compromise may be the answer. Discussion with both parents and a third party may lead to a way of resolving disagreements between parents.

In much of the Code concerning parents the emphasis is understandably on the parents representing their own child's interests as they see them. There are circum-stances in which parents seek to represent the interests of other parents whose children have SEN. In such instances (and SEN fora are one example) the contribution of parents is valuable where they draw on personal experience in a general way (and that of other parents reported to them) to contribute to debate and policy decision-making.

The three question reconsidered

Earlier in this chapter, three questions were posed and each will now be examined.

Which groups have a legitimate interest in SEN and therefore a 'right' to represent interests of children with SEN?

This chapter considered children themselves, disability lobby groups and parents. The involvement of children in their education may be either direct, by discussing matters with them, or through advocacy.

Disability interest groups can contribute effectively so long as it is not unquestion-ingly assumed that representatives necessarily have privileged experience or knowledge of the particular aspects and issues of SEN that are being discussed. A repre-sentative of a disability interest group may, of course, have such experience and knowledge but, equally, he may not.

Parents have statutory rights to represent the interests of their children but it is not always easy to judge the extent to which a parent is representing a child or, in a forum, the extent to which one parent represents other parents.

The supposed 'right' to represent what is considered to be the interests of the child with SEN should be assumed with some humility and considerable care.

What weight should be placed on the respective views of participants?

With reference to an SEN forum, it seems sensible to judge the question of the weight applied to respective views not in the forum itself, but in the process by which the forum is constituted.

It is therefore important that some discussion takes place about the forms of representation that are being drawn on, however imperfect these forms may be. Are representatives chosen for their good education and/or their wide experience? Are they regarded as mandated? Are they present because of some form of characteristic representation? Or is there an uneasy mixture of these models with particular aspects of representation coming to the fore or being claimed by representatives at different times and in relation to different issues? Whatever the form of representation, it is important that the forum has the confidence of those it purports to represent.

However members of a forum represent others, there should be ways of ensuring, as far as practicable, that representatives can discuss matters with those they represent. Even if the representative does not consider herself to be absolutely bound by mandate, but makes up her own mind about matters, knowledge of the views of those she represents can still inform the process of developing views.

The implications of all this is that, once people are members of a forum, they have an equally valued voice within that forum. Extra weight is not placed on a view because it comes from a child advocate or a member of a disability lobby or a parent or anyone else.

Where views differ, what is the mechanism for seeking to resolve differences?

In one sense, the mechanism for resolving differences is the forum itself and the consultation and reflection that takes place outside it. Different views are aired, debated and balanced against other views.

Sometimes, the officers representing the LEA, the health service or the social services will be responsible for making decisions with which all members of the forum cannot agree. Even in such instances, the forum can enable the person making the decision to be better informed than she might otherwise have been. At this point, the focus of issues begins to concern power as well as representation, and power is the subject of the chapter in this volume, 'Parent, LEA and SENDIST: balance of power'.

Case study

An SEN forum

The Devon Parent Partnership Service involves six home-based part-time paid workers (Development Workers) providing guidance and support to parents and carers (hereafter 'parents'). There are plans to recruit and train volunteers (Independent Parental Supporters) to assist this work. The Development Workers operate in the six Primary Care Trust (PCT) localities across the Devon authority. The PCT areas are: Exeter, East Devon, Mid Devon, North Devon, Teignbridge, and South Hams and West Devon. Development Workers' knowledge is mainly in the area of SEN but in recognition of the multi-service requirements of children with SEN, they are expanding their knowledge to incorporate multi-disciplinary concerns and extending working relationships and contacts with health and social service personnel.

The service comprises two strands: a support and training service and a mechanism to allow parents to become involved in policy.

Parent volunteers, in conjunction with Devon Education Authority and the Devon Parent Partnership Service have established a framework for the operation of fora. There is a county forum and several locality fora.

The **county forum** is 'owned' and led by parents and its membership comprises parents and staff representatives from statutory agencies whom the parent representatives have agreed should be invited. There are two parent members from each of the six Primary Care Trust (PCT) localities, who are democratically selected by their locality, and they may use a rota system to ensure at least one parent attends meetings. The invited members of the statutory services are senior officers from the health, social and education services, and joint agency managers also attend. Speakers are invited to the forum as appropriate.

The county forum was established at the request of parents to enable them to be informed, consulted and involved in the national and local planning of services. It aims to ensure that the opinions of parents are heard from across the county. In line with the Special Educational Needs Code of Practice, 2002, the forum provides a means of communication between parents and statutory agencies. It aims to monitor county-wide contracts, such as respite services, and to involve parents in developing practice and policy.

County Forum meetings are held six times a year, rotating between the three locations of Exeter, Tiverton and Newton Abbot. Each venue is adjacent to the three localities where meetings are not currently held to ensure that members can attend as easily as possible in a large rural county. The minutes of the meetings are circulated to a wide range of parents, carers and professionals, and those who cannot attend receive information that has been provided at the meetings. The minutes also appear on the Parent Partnership Service website. A liaison officer assists with raising particular issues with senior officers in the education, health or social services. However, the chairperson often discusses matters directly with the relevant senior professionals.

Locality fora were formed in order to extend the work of the county forum into each area of Devon. They provide the means of a dialogue between representatives on the county forum and representatives of the statutory agencies that attend the county forum. They deal with matters that are more specific to their particular locality and feed these back to the county forum. They also provide an opportunity for parents in a local area to be involved in the 'bigger picture' by highlighting local issues which are then represented at the county forum, and county forum matters are relayed back to the localities.

Statutory agencies in the six PCT localities welcome parents' involvement in the planning of future services and value their views. The fora are not used to air any personal grievances of parents as these are addressed through other channels (notably the support and advisory section of the Parent Partnership Service and other specialist support groups). However, where a parent's personal experience informs judgement about local services and raises issues that need to be addressed, these are welcomed.

Parents in each locality forum have the opportunity to develop it in a way that reflects the distinctive nature of each locality and, while each has autonomy, each has a responsibility to support the county forum. Representatives must report back to the parents in the localities. Designated funds have been set aside to assist parents travelling, but there is no designated funding to help directly with childcare expenses, although parents receive an hourly rate to attend county forum meetings.

It is recognised that the success of the fora relates to up-to-date and reliable information about any proposed changes being provided to the county forum from the three services (social, health, education). This is done through the professional representatives who are invited to the forum providing either written or spoken accounts of proposals or by means of consultation papers and by parents responding accordingly. Professionals will also visit the locality fora so that consultation issues can be clearly presented and understood by all, and to provide an opportunity for parents and carers to ask questions.

Areas for future development include:

- to develop a clearer definition of the Development Workers' roles in relation to the locality fora;
- to extend their joint working with the joint agency teams; and
- to seek ways to promote awareness of the Parent Partnership Service and the fora to include a wider range of parents.

Efforts are constantly being made to extend participation in the fora. Not all parents wish to attend formal meetings and one possible approach could be a chatroom on a Parent Partnership website. However, this would reach only parents having access to the internet. It is important that parents and carers know who their representative is so that they can pass on issues for discussion through them to the locality and county fora.

(From information kindly supplied by Devon County Council and the Devon Parent Partnership Service)

Summary/conclusion

Arrangements for ascertaining the views of children with SEN, either directly or through child advocacy, were considered. Related to these arrangements (and sometimes supplementing them) are ways in which groups seek to represent the views and/or interests of children with SEN. These include disability interest groups and parents' groups.

The SEN forum is one way of representing the views of parents of children having SEN, therefore representing their children in a general way both locally and nationally. The strength of such an approach includes opportunities for parents to enter into a dialogue with members of the social, education and health services and others to debate issues and inform decision-making on policy.

Particularly if the problematic nature of representation is borne in mind, the contribution of parents and others to special educational policy is likely to strengthen policy and help build commitment to the policies themselves.

As a mechanism for bringing together different views, the forum, while it has limitations, may form a basis for gradually developing consensus around complex issues in special education including the development of services for children with SEN.

7

Educating Pupils with Profound and Multiple Learning Difficulties: Rationality and Autonomy

INTRODUCTION

Morality that is too earnest can be a source of ridicule, as when George Bernard Shaw in Pygmalion has Pickering ask Mr Doolittle, 'Do you have no morals man?' Doolittle replies, 'Can't afford them governor'. But a considered moral response to the issue considered in this chapter, that of reason and free will in relation to educating pupils with profound and multiple learning difficulties (PMLD), seems necessary and appropriate.

This chapter outlines the general understanding of the notions of 'reason' and of 'free will' in terms of liberal theory. It suggests that liberal theory is weak in offering protection to people with PMLD to the extent that people with PMLD are considered to have, to a very limited degree, the powers of reason and free will that constitute a moral person in liberal theory. The moral convictions and motives of parents who care for children with PMLD are considered.

Those who educate children with PMLD, it is suggested, may be motivated by moral convictions similar to those of parents of children with PMLD and by other convictions. It is argued that teachers and others may not use considerations of rationality and free will as justifications for their commitment to teaching these children. However, these educators still value the powers of rationality and free will as expressed in their attempts to encourage these in pupils. This is reflected in curricula and approaches to teaching and learning considered suitable for pupils with PMLD.

A case study illustrates how in teaching pupils with PMLD, teachers and schools assume that pupils can be initiated into an approach to the curriculum that embodies rationality.

Reason and free will in liberal theory

The noun 'reason' can be defined in several ways as indicated by the definitions in the *Concise Oxford Dictionary*. It is 'the intellectual faculty by which conclusions are drawn from premises'. In philosophical terms, a 'premise' is the position from which an 'argument', or course of reasoning, starts. Any argument must begin from at least one premise, and this is assumed, so that the argument does not have to prove the premise before it starts. The argument is valid if it proves that its conclusions follow from its premise. But this does not prove that the conclusions are true – something that an argument cannot demonstrate.

A further definition is that the noun 'reason' is 'a faculty transcending the understanding and providing a priori principles; intuition'. In philosophy, a priori is something known to be valid before experience, in contrast to 'a posteriori', which is something the validity of which can only be determined by experience. Reason, in this light, provides principles that are valid in advance of experience.

The verb 'reason' is defined as to 'form or try to reach conclusions by connected thought', and to 'express in a logical or argumentative form'. The term 'reason', it can be seen, even when used in this more general way, relates to 'argument' or 'connected thought'.

In general usage, as also reflected in the definition given in the *Concise Oxford Dictionary*, 'free will' is 'the power of acting without the constraint or necessity of fate' or 'the ability to act at one's own discretion'. A related concept is that of autonomy, which involves 'personal freedom' and 'freedom of the will'.

Liberal thought has been typified by a 'commitment to individualism', that is a conviction that the human individual is of supreme importance (Haywood 1999: 29). This implies strong support for individual freedom. Individuals are regarded as 'rational creatures' entitled to 'the greatest possible freedom' that is consistent with a similar freedom for other citizens. Whereas classical liberalism tended to regard freedom in so-called negative terms as the lack of outside constraints on the individual, modern liberalism holds a 'positive' view of freedom linked to 'personal development and self-realisation' (ibid.: 29). The virtue of liberalism is seen as its 'unrelenting commitment to individual freedom, reasoned debate and toleration' (ibid.: 33).

Liberal theory gives a moral framework for guiding interactions between free, equal, rational and reasonable human beings. The moral conception of the individual in liberal theory is based on the capacities of human beings as 'moral agents' using capacities such as 'the powers of reason and free will' (Reinders 2000: 105). Also, it is a feature of liberal theory that all citizens deserve to be treated with equal concern and respect.

Moral status and the inclusion of people with PMLD

Having outlined the central importance to liberal thought of the notions of rationality and freedom, one can examine this in relation to people with PMLD in terms of moral status. Moral status in this context refers to the ability of someone as a moral agent to understand right and wrong.

When discrimination was discussed in the chapter 'School equal opportunity policies: equality and discrimination', it was suggested that the understanding of discrimination as related to trying to treat people equally (and provide equality of opportunity) is problematic. Another approach was indicated, that of regarding discrimination as treating a person with undeserved contempt, although this was not without its difficulties. Even the preferred position of trying to ensure that people were in a 'good enough' position still required further clarification.

A view put forward by Reinders relates to treating people unequally, but it refers also to doing this in terms of 'morally irrelevant' characteristics. In certain circumstances, this may be the equivalent of treating a person with unjustified contempt. Reinders, then, believes that to discriminate against someone is 'to ignore their capacity as human agents by treating them unequally on grounds of morally irrelevant characteristics' (ibid.: 106). Such morally irrelevant characteristics include race, sex, religion and age. But what of PMLD?

When a person is considered to have PMLD, their degree of learning difficulty is such that they are functioning at a developmental level of two years or less. As Ware (2003: v) points out, in practice the developmental level is often well under a year. Also, a person with PMLD may have one or more other severe impairments such as visual impairment or very limited mobility, further limiting their learning.

It follows that, at a certain level of severity, a child with PMLD lacks or has to a very limited degree the powers of reason and the capacity to exert free will. Reinders (*op. cit.*: 106–7), referring to people with 'the more profound varieties of mental disabilities' (ibid.: 107), states that: 'they do not possess the powers of *reason* and *free will*; they oftentimes cannot give an account of why they do what they do, nor can they make plans for the future, given the fact that they lack a sense of time. Consequently, their behaviour hardly counts as human action understood as *intentionally directed* and guided by *reason*' (ibid.: 106–7, italics added).

However, if PMLD affects the person's 'capacity for human agency' (ibid.: 106), then liberal theory suggests that PMLD *is* a morally relevant characteristic that allows unequal treatment. Liberal theory is therefore weak in offering protection against discrimination for people with PMLD.

Given that the status of persons is an important moral concern, where someone falls outside the scope of liberal morality they are included indirectly. Accordingly, infants are included because of their potentiality to become moral agents in the future and the inclusion of 'profoundly mentally disabled' people is taken to depend on the interests of their relatives (ibid.: 23). However, Reinders maintains that the liberal convention fails to include, on the basis of equality, people with PMLD (whom he refers to as people with profound mental disabilities). He argues:

> people with mental disabilities are lacking to a greater or lesser extent the powers of reason and free will. Since these are the powers that bring substance to the core values of the liberal view on public morality, mentally disabled people never acquire full moral standing in this view. This is because its moral community is constituted by 'persons' and these, in turn, are constituted by the powers of reason and free will. This conception of the person is particularly problematic with respect to the inclusion of mentally disabled citizens, since, on the liberal view, only persons in the sense of rational moral agents can be the recipients of equal concern and respect. (ibid.: 15–16, italics added)

The view outlined above, particularly in expressions such as 'their behaviour hardly counts as human action' and 'capacity for human agency', seems to suggest that in liberal theory there are degrees or levels of being human. There is an assumption that being more intelligent equates with being more human. However, it is also possible to regard the differences between a person with PMLD and those of others who do not have learning difficulties as to some extent quantitative (rather than exclusively qualitative). It may also be worth remembering that people who do not experience learning difficulties are not considered totally reasonable (if such a state can be imagined). This is a matter of degree also and it may be said of everyone that, 'to a greater or lesser degree', they lack powers of reason and free will.

Participation in the democratic process

In practical terms, participation in the democratic process, such as casting a democratic vote for a political party, cannot be meaningful, given that people with PMLD often have a developmental level of well under a year. For example, in the context of citizenship initiatives, consideration has been given to post-16 citizenship teaching and learning, including helping young people with learning difficulties/disabilities to use their democratic vote. Pavey (2003) worries that, 'pupils with moderate and severe learning difficulties' who are educated in mainstream school may only be thought capable of a lower aspiring 'special' citizenship education (ibid.: 59). Even in arguing strongly for developing the political awareness of such students, Pavey (2003) appears to accept limits, stating:

> While it is difficult to think of the most severely learning disabled students as able to comprehend difficult concepts, there are many more who might well be able to achieve at least a partial understanding of political issues, if the attempt were made. Even severely learning disabled people are entitled, and able, to make simple but important choices about how they live their lives, with appropriate support. (ibid.: 62–3)

The only people over the age of 18 years who *as a group* do not have a right to vote are peers of the realm, convicted prisoners and the clinically insane. But, if a presiding officer considers that any individual is unable to understand the voting process, he may not issue a ballot paper to that person. In such cases, the presiding officer asks two prescribed questions which must be answered satisfactorily before the ballot paper is issued. The first question is whether the person is the person registered on the electoral register under that name. The answer to this question has to be affirmative. The second question is whether the person has already voted, other than as a proxy for someone else. The answer to this question has to be negative.

As Pavey points out, these are quite simple questions that, hopefully, can be delivered in simple language. She suggests that as questions 'they can be answered by a *great many* of those with learning disabilities' (ibid.: 63, italics added). Again, there is an implicit acceptance that for those with the most severe learning difficulties such questions would not be understood. I am assuming that these are learners who, when younger and in school, would be pupils having PMLD.

It is suggested that people with PMLD lack 'to a greater or lesser degree the powers of reason and free will' (Reinders 2000: 15), and, in practical terms, are unable to understand and participate in the machinery of democracy, such as voting for a political party. If this is so, then the inclusion of people with PMLD cannot be publicly justified in a direct way without introducing convictions and beliefs that go beyond the public domain as it is understood in liberal theory. The extent that people with PMLD are included in a liberal democracy must therefore depend on something other than the weak support offered by liberal theory.

Moral convictions and motives for caring for dependent others

Reinders suggests that if we ignore facts about our moral convictions, we ignore facts about the integrity of our moral self that can be dismissed only 'at the cost of impairing that self' (Reinders 2000: 123). Secondly, Reinders argues that the moral standing of people with PMLD reflects a particular way of how we understand the relationship we share with them. For a parent to accept responsibility for sharing their lives with a child with PMLD and therefore to accept responsibility for the relationship in which he finds himself, is not an object of choice and decision. It is 'constituitive' of the moral self (ibid.: 125).

One does not accept responsibility for children with PMLD because one has a reciprocal relationship with them in terms of a social contract. A basis for accepting responsibility could be that one sees the dependent person as given to us in the sense that 'prior to the rules and principles of social morality, the presence of the other in our lives constitutes our responsibility' (ibid.: 17). Moral responsibility, therefore, arises from the nature of the moral self which 'discovers itself within a network of social relationships' (ibid.: 17). Only when we regard our own lives as received from others that have accepted responsibility for us, will we be able to support dependent others who cannot reciprocate our actions.

Moral convictions and motives in educating children with PMLD

The valuing of children with PMLD by teachers and others that work with them may be informed by similar commitments to those that motivate parents. Of course, teachers and others who educate children with PMLD do not 'find themselves' in a relationship with a child with PMLD in the same way that a parent does. Teachers choose to work with the children. However, their continuation in the work and the fact that many are able to find satisfaction in working with pupils with PMLD may be explained in a similar way to the commitment of parents.

Moral convictions in relation to the importance of interactions and communication are expressed for example by Favell *et al.* (1996), where it is suggested that the happiness of some individuals with PMLD can be increased by interventions in interactions. Ware (2003), after explaining the approach of creating a 'responsive environment' (this is touched on later in this chapter) and outlining its importance in terms of its potential to develop communication, social interaction, social development and learning, suggests a further paramount reason for its importance. This is that the approach manifests the 'respect and dignity' (ibid.: 3) with which all people, whatever their abilities or disabilities, 'ought to be treated'. It teaches us that we are 'valued and respected' (ibid.: 13).

Rationality and autonomy and the education of children with PMLD

Educating pupils with PMLD is informed by a valuing of rationality and not by a devaluing of children with PMLD because of limitations of their rationality. The valuing of rationality is evident in the efforts made to identify and encourage and develop rationality and greater autonomy through the curriculum and other means.

For example, guidance for *Planning, Teaching and Assessing the Curriculum for Pupils with Learning Difficulties* has been developed which includes general guidelines (Qualifications and Curriculum Authority and the Department for Education and Employment 2001). They relate to pupils having moderate learning difficulties (who may be achieving within age-related expectations in some subjects but are well below this in others). They also apply to pupils with severe and profound and multiple learning difficulties. The guidance indicates these pupils are unlikely to achieve above level 2 at the end of Key Stage 4 of the National Curriculum, that is they are unlikely to achieve at the level of most children of 11 when they are 16 years old (ibid.: 4). In fact, for pupils with PMLD, the level of achievement is likely to be lower than this and the guidance indicates that it includes a framework to help teachers recognise achievement 'below level 1 of the National Curriculum' (ibid.: 1). Integral to these subject guidelines are small steps performance descriptors (P scales) that help assess and record what the pupil has attained.

Among the aims for a curriculum for pupils with learning difficulties are ones that can clearly be associated with encouraging rationality and free will. For example, the curriculum might aim to: 'enable pupils to express *preferences*, communicate needs, make *choices*, make *decisions* and choose *options* that other people act on and respect'; 'prepare pupils for an adult life in which they have the greatest possible degree of *autonomy*, and support them in having relationships with mutual respect and dependence on each other' (ibid.: 6, italics added).

Therapy can also contribute to 'promoting pupils' *autonomy* and *independence* through the use of specialist aids and equipment' (ibid.: 8, italics added).

Very small steps in progress towards rational and autonomous responses are recognised in such ways as when pupils 'develop a range of responses to actions, events or experiences even if there is no clear progress in acquiring knowledge and skills'. Or pupils may 'demonstrate a reduced need for support, for example from another person, from technology, from individualised equipment, in carrying out particular tasks' (ibid.: 22).

A framework intended to help teachers recognise attainment below level 1 of the National Curriculum is expressed in terms of encounter, awareness, attention and response, engagement, participation, involvement, and gaining skills and understanding. For example, 'encounter' refers to pupils being present during an experience or activity without any obvious learning outcome, although for some pupils, such as 'those who withhold their attention or their presence from many situations, their willingness to tolerate a shared activity may, in itself, be significant' (ibid.: 27).

As well as the content of curriculum frameworks, various approaches indicate the value placed on encouraging progress in learning for children with PMLD. For example, as mentioned earlier, a range of approaches is brought together under the term 'responsive environment' (Ware 2003). A responsive environment in the context of the present chapter is one in which pupils with PMLD 'get responses to their actions, get the opportunity to give responses to the actions of others, and have the opportunity to take the lead in interaction' (ibid.: 1). Such an environment is considered important for social, intellectual and communicative development.

The approaches of alternative and augmentative communication are further interesting developments. While the former are used in the place of speech, the latter support speech. Collectively, these systems are referred to as augmentative and alternative communication (AAL). Augmentative communication has been described as 'an approach which is clearly an addition to speech or writing', and alternative communication has been defined as 'a substitute for (or alternative to) natural speech and/or handwriting' (Lloyd and Blischak 1992). The systems may include the use of manual signing systems such as 'Makaton' or 'Signalong', objects of reference, and other tactile symbols such as Braille (Hendrickson 1997). Where a child does not go on to use spoken language sufficiently proficiently, these forms may later offer the main means of communication or may be used to support continuing attempts at spoken communication.

As is pointed out by McLinden and McCall (2002: 114), AAL systems use a representation such as letters, words, graphic symbols, pictures or objects. Or they may involve speech units usually recorded and initiated using an electronic device. Writing about children with visual impairment and additional difficulties, McLinden and McCall draw out the distinction between visual symbols, such as a photograph or a printed word, and tactile symbols, such as objects of reference, raised pictorial symbols and Braille.

In the context of curricular frameworks and in approaches to teaching and learning for pupils with PMLD, the notions of rationality and autonomy form an important underpinning.

Case study: Curriculum approaches in a school for pupils with PMLD

The following extracts are adapted from a school document setting out the provision for children with PMLD. The school is St Luke's Primary Special School, North Lincolnshire, and the extracts are used with the kind permission of the head teacher Dr Rob Ashdown.

Provision for children who have profound and multiple learning difficulties

The focus of this document is a group of pupils who are usually described as having PMLD and who constitute an increasing proportion (currently about 25%) of the pupil population in St Luke's Primary Special School.

If we are to be successful in meeting the highly individual needs of these children, it is necessary to be aware of the implications of their learning difficulties, albeit in general terms. Our problem is that we have difficulty in understanding what the world must seem like to them precisely because of their language and cognitive problems.

Even though the organs of the senses may be intact, some children with PMLD can show inconsistent reactions to stimuli. When stimuli are presented at normal levels the child may show little or no reaction or may overreact and show signs of distress or panic. This is particularly true of some children with autism who often also seem to be unable to cope with irregularities in their environment such as changes from the normal classroom routines or new people in the room. Therefore it is essential that teachers plan to create new areas in classrooms with minimal distractions and to avoid a lot of free activity and high levels of noise or types of noise which provoke anxiety.

The pupils experience difficulties with memory and with maintaining attention. To a certain extent these problems may be minimised by slowing down the rate of presentation of stimuli, allowing sufficient time for a response or using prompts and cues to draw attention to the relevant stimuli. The pupils often experience great difficulty in using spontaneously learned skills and knowledge outside the original teaching setting. Therefore educational theory emphasises the value of over-learning and explicitly planning to teach the use of learned skills in naturalistic settings beyond the original teaching situation.

The teacher has to structure the learning environment so that it is largely predictable and non-threatening, but a certain degree of challenge must be introduced in a carefully controlled fashion. If the child fails, the teacher should help by providing clear cues and demonstrations of alternative and more appropriate responses.

The communication and language skills of these children are very seriously delayed ... It falls to their teachers, parents and carers to put great effort into developing communication exchanges by responding as though these children are communicating with intent and thus show them that their behaviour can have an influence on the people around them. Reciprocal interaction is encouraged when adults are responsive, behave in interesting and enjoyable ways, and when they allow time for pupils to respond and prompt this if no response is forthcoming.

'Total communication' is advocated rather than a reliance on speech alone, and therefore signs, symbols, gestures, photographs and objects all have their place as part of a non-vocal augmentative system for communication. Systematic use might be made of touch cues so that pupils with visual impairments come to learn that a touch cue to a particular part of the body has a specific meaning; for example, that it is time for a drink or time to go to the toilet. Teachers must ensure that there are reasons for pupils to communicate, and therefore it is vitally important that adults should not always anticipate and provide for all their wants. Indeed, teachers may engineer situations where children have to communicate their need, perhaps for something that has been hidden or placed out of the child's reach.

Implementing interventions requires considerable planning, the deliberate use of prompts, cues and special reinforcers, and a graded approach to change. Programmes may be introduced gradually. For instance, the initial focus of an intervention might be on one setting, and gradually the intervention can be extended to other settings. Alternatively, the intervention may target only one form of challenging behaviour at first, and may subsequently be extended to other challenging behaviours one at a time. Above all, parents, carers and teachers must work to achieve a consensus view about the nature of the intervention and its goals.

The following curriculum entitlements, which form shared entitlements for all pupils, are relevant for pupils with PMLD:

- curriculum guidance for the foundation stage for pupils in the first years of their education;

- the general requirements in the National Curriculum and, in particular, the statement on inclusion which sets out requirements under three broad principles (setting suitable learning challenges; responding to pupils' diverse learning needs; and overcoming potential barriers to learning and assessment for individual pupils and groups of pupils);

- the full range of subjects of the National Curriculum including religious education, sex and relationships education, and other aspects of personal, health and social education according to the relevant key stage; and

- provision which prepares pupils for adult life.

All children should be provided with opportunities to acquire, develop, practise, apply and extend their skills in a range of contexts across the curriculum. These skills will also be relevant to life and learning outside and beyond the school.

The six skill areas embedded in the National Curriculum subjects relate to:

- communication, including the application of literacy skills;

- application of number;

- information technology;

- working with others;

- improving own learning and performance; and

- problem-solving.

'Thinking skills' complement the six key skills and are embedded in the National Curriculum. Thinking skills include 'sensory awareness' and 'perception skills' and range of 'early thinking skills' such as predicting and anticipating, remembering, the understanding of cause and effect, linking objects, events and experiences, and thinking creatively and imaginatively.

Additional priorities relate to:

- physical, orientation and mobility skills;

- organisation and study skills;

- personal and social skills, including personal care skills and managing own behaviour and emotions;

- leisure and recreational skills; and

- daily living skills, including domestic skills and community skills.

The development of these skills is an important part of the curriculum. Opportunities for the development of the skills should be highlighted in curriculum planning across the whole range of subjects and in children's individual education plans (IEPs).

The National Curriculum is a major part of the whole curriculum of the school. It has to be taught in a way that is appropriate to the age, interests and needs of each child. IEPs will also influence the way in which the curriculum is delivered and the choice of learning targets for IEPs will continue to be made in consultation with parents and other interested parties, taking into account children's interests and preferences where these can be ascertained.

The National Curriculum describes definite national targets for all children aged between 5 and 16 years and specifies the educational programmes required to meet these targets at several stages of education.

The government introduced the National Curriculum with the needs of all pupils in mind. It is our job at this school to ensure that it is taught in ways that are relevant to the pupils here and that meet their special educational needs.

Medium-term plans take the form of units of work organised according to a long-term plan for each subject. Units of work have been written in such a way as to provide opportunities for all pupils to make progress. However, there is also specific time allocation for activities aimed at promoting aspects of development which are additional to the National Curriculum such as hydrotherapy, interactive communication and mobility (through the Mobility Opportunities Via Education Programme).

Summary/conclusion

This chapter considered the argument that liberal thinking is weak in offering protection to people with PMLD to the extent that people with PMLD are considered to have, to a lesser degree than usual, the powers of reason and free will that constitute a moral person in liberal theory. Those who educate children with PMLD may be motivated by moral beliefs similar to those of parents of children with PMLD and by other convictions. Teachers and others involved in the education of these children may not use considerations of rationality and free will as they apply to individual children as justifications for their commitment to these children. However, these educators value the powers of rationality and free will as expressed in their attempts to encourage these in pupils reflected in curricula and approaches to teaching and learning considered suitable for pupils with PMLD. A case study illustrated how, in teaching pupils with PMLD, teachers and schools assume that pupils can be initiated into a rational approach to the curriculum.

8

Including Pupils with SEN: Rights and Duties

INTRODUCTION

William Hepworth Thompson said of Richard Jebb, later to become Professor of Greek at Cambridge, 'Such time as he can spare from the adornment of his person he devotes to the neglect of his duties'. But, while duties may not always be taken seriously, they can sometimes clarify the nature and remit of related 'rights'.

As this chapter concerns the 'rights' associated with inclusion, I first explain the particular aspect of inclusion under consideration. I examine what inclusion is (or more accurately, what I am focusing on for the purpose of this chapter). In specifying what aspect of inclusion is being discussed, I will explain who I am referring to and where the inclusion would take place. The chapter then looks at why inclusion might be justified, how it might take place and when.

The chapter concentrates on legal rights, outlining four types. I then consider examples of legal rights in special education: the right to be educated in the mainstream and the civil rights of disabled pupils relating to inclusion. The duties of the local education authority and others are considered to clarify the nature of the inclusion 'right' and the rights of others that compete with inclusion rights are examined. Both of these indicate the boundaries on 'right' to inclusion.

A case study examines the efforts of an LEA model of behaviour support balancing the right of a pupil with SEN to be educated in mainstream with related duties of the LEA and the school. This is done through a progressive approach to supporting pupils with behavioural, emotional and social difficulties in mainstream schools and identifying a clear role for special schools.

Inclusion – Who, What, Where?

Inclusion, is a seductive word sounding self-evidently positive, encouraging everyone to subscribe to it. This is reinforced by its opposite, 'exclusion', which at first glance seems to hold negative connotations. Yet inclusion is not always positive, as anyone not wishing to be 'included' in a gang planning to rob a bank, or in an expedition through the Gobi Desert might testify.

Whether or not it is positive to be included in anything depends in what one is being included and who is being included. In an educational context, the 'who' aspect may relate to children and young people considered at risk of social exclusion. This approach to social inclusion is reflected in such documents as Circular 10/99 (Department for Education and Employment 1999a) and Circular 11/99 Department for Education and Employment 1999b). Circular 10/99 mentions that among children at risk of exclusion from school are those with SEN who develop challenging behaviour. Circular 11/99 indicates that LEAs consider legal remedies to compel the attendance of non-attending pupils. The inclusion of some of these children may involve providing education in a pupil support unit or pupil referral unit.

The 'who' may refer to pupils already in mainstream schools, as seems to be the case with the *Index for Inclusion* (Booth *et al*. 2000). A focus on these children involves developing a culture for inclusion in these schools. This implies encouraging schools to reconsider their structure, teaching approaches, pupil grouping and use of support so that they respond to the diverse learning needs of all their pupils. According to the *Index*, drawing on experimentation and reflection, teachers need to develop opportunities to look at new ways of involving all pupils. The school needs to provide planned access to a broad and balanced curriculum, developed from its foundations as a curriculum for all pupils. Teachers in these schools are likely to hold values supporting inclusive practice, believing that pupils with SEN belong in mainstream classes. There will be a commitment both to reviewing performance and to change. Collaborative problem-solving is used to seek solutions to challenges arising when teaching a diverse group of pupils. Teachers draw on various instructional approaches.

Sometimes the 'who' of inclusion is very broad (and this is related to what inclusion is considered to be). For example, in the document (Office for Standards in Education 2000) inclusion applies to:

- boys and girls;
- minority ethnic and faith groups, travellers, asylum seekers and refugees;
- pupils who need support to learn English as an additional language;
- pupils with SEN;
- gifted and talented pupils;

- children who are 'looked after' by the local authority;

- sick children;

- young carers;

- children from families under stress;

- pregnant schoolgirls;

- teenage mothers; and

- pupils who are at risk of disaffection or exclusion.

The potential difficulty with such a broad approach is that in its breadth (include everybody) any particular considerations that concern or affect a particular group may not receive sufficient attention.

For this reason, this chapter concentrates on the inclusion of pupils with severe or complex SEN (almost invariably having a statement of SEN) that might be thought to justify their education in a special school/unit. When I mention pupils with SEN subsequently in this present chapter, it is to these pupils that I am referring, not to pupils considered to have SEN presently in mainstream schools.

The 'who' aspect of inclusion also helps to refine what inclusion is intended to mean in this chapter. If we return to the point about positive or negative perspectives of inclusion, depending on what one is included in, then this refers, in the present context, to education provided in a mainstream school classroom.

Precisely then, I am concerned with the balance of pupils with severe/complex SEN in mainstream or special schools. The word 'balance' pre-judges certain issues and it may be maintained that the correct 'balance' should be that all pupils are educated in mainstream schools. This will be considered when I examine 'why' inclusion should be encouraged. Also, it is not always a matter of a pupil being educated only in a mainstream school or only in a special school. Sometimes the pupil may be educated for part of the time in mainstream and part of the time in special school. The issues, about which is the preferred venue are similar whether one is considering either/or the proportion of time that a particular pupil spends in either mainstream or special school. That is, both concern the valuing of education in a mainstream or in a special school. This is the *where* aspect of inclusion.

It was the above aspect that was the concern of the government Green Paper, *Excellence for All Children: Meeting Special Educational Needs* (Department for Education 1997), concerning raising standards, shifting resources to practical support and increasing inclusion. The document stated that:

The ultimate purpose of SEN provision is to enable young people to flourish in adult life. There are therefore strong educational, as well as social and moral, grounds for educating children with SEN with their peers. We aim to increase the level and quality of inclusion within mainstream schools, while protecting and enhancing specialist provision for those who need it. (p. 43)

Why inclusion?

The question, *why* encourage inclusion? now arises. Specifically, one can ask why it might be considered desirable for a pupil with SEN to be educated wholly or predominantly in a mainstream school rather than a special school.

The *social* reasons might be that a pupil with SEN will develop better socially and personally in a mainstream school rather than a special school. Such a belief is sometimes presented by identifying the child's peers as pupils in mainstream schools rather than pupils in special schools but this seems to beg the question of who the child's peers are. It is not made clear, when such views are expressed, why a child educated in a special school with pupils of the same age who also have similar SEN is not considered to be with peers.

The *educational* reasons for inclusion in mainstream might be that the educational progress that a child makes and the standards of attainment and achievement reached would be higher in a mainstream school than in a special school. This concerns cognitive development to the extent that this can be considered separately from social and personal development. Such a view seems to have been that of Thomas (1997) in his interpretation of examination results in mainstream and special schools. Unfortunately, this interpretation is not supportable on the evidence Thomas considers because the progress of pupils starting from a comparable baseline was not taken into account. (For a fuller consideration see Farrell 2004: 40.)

A *moral* reason for including a child in a mainstream school rather than a special school might be that special schools may seem to be oppressive because they segregate pupils with SEN. If segregation were the only moral objection to special schooling, or even one objection to it, then it would be difficult to justify many other kinds of separation such as that of boys and girls, pupils with particular talents in 'specialist' schools and different cultural and religious groups (Christian, Muslim, Jewish schools). However, the term 'segregation' perhaps implies something that 'separation' does not. One might have separate schools for different religious groups, talented pupils, and for boys and girls, but one might regard the separate schools for pupils with SEN as segregated rather than separated. Perhaps the term 'segregation' implies enforced separation for a malign reason.

For those suspecting a malign motive for separating pupils with SEN, the fact that other groups are separate may not carry much weight. However, to maintain such a view would necessitate identifying and demonstrating what the malign motive in relation to pupils with SEN might be. Otherwise, to object to special schools simply because they offer separate education would require anyone holding such a view to reject the separate education of gender and religious groups.

The Report of the Special Schools Working Group (Department for Education and Skills 2003b) confirms the continuation of special schools. Naturally, many special schools will continue to educate pupils who will also spend some time in mainstream schools.

Perhaps the *moral* argument for inclusion is informed by the social and educational justifications of mainstream inclusion. If a child makes slower progress and reaches lower standards of attainment and lower levels of social and personal development when attending a special school, then this may contribute to the moral view that the child should attend a mainstream school.

Another aspect of the moral case for inclusion may be that, if pupils with the most severe SEN are educated in special schools, then pupils in mainstream schools would be less likely to have any kind of contact with such pupils. They might, therefore, be less likely to include pupils with SEN in their friendship groups, for example, perhaps affecting their social contacts later in life. Such a consideration might inform the education of a child with SEN for some of the time in mainstream school so long as this did not impede the academic, social and personal development that the child might make in special school.

Inclusion – How?

If a mainstream school is to provide a better education than a special school, then the *how* of inclusion is important. The mainstream school can seek to extend the range of pupils with SEN that it educates by developing:

- flexibility in the curriculum;
- flexibility in assessment;
- flexibility in pedagogy; and
- flexibility in school organisation.

(Farrell 2004: 131–48)

Inclusion – When?

When the inclusion of pupils with SEN takes place is the final question. If one believes that inclusion is a process, then the answer to when? is probably 'all the time'. But the notion of a process ducks the issue of what inclusion really is. A process has to have an ultimate end-point even if this is never reached and this gives it its sense of direction, unless one is speaking of a circular process such as the rain-cycle. But if the goal is not specified, then a process view of inclusion lacks clarity, if not meaning.

If one considers inclusion with reference to including pupils with SEN in mainstream rather than in special schools, then views of when this may be appropriate can be seen in terms of the earlier outline of moral, social and educational reasons for inclusion.

The moral drive for inclusion, then, arises when a special school is less successful than a mainstream school in encouraging the development of a child educationally and socially. This can be (and already is in some LEAs) informed by judgements about particular special schools (see Farrell 2004: 41–3). The corollary is that, when a special school is more successful in aiding educational and social development, then this provides a moral consideration for educating the child in a special school.

It will be seen that this is rather like a 'bottom up' approach to inclusion in which it is informed by the effect on real children in real schools. It is not the 'top down' approach regarding inclusion in a mainstream school as a morally self-evidently positive course to pursue.

In practical terms, the balance of inclusion in mainstream school will be influenced by two factors. First, it will be influenced by the degree of flexibility which mainstream schools can create in the curriculum, assessment, pedagogy and organisation that will ensure progress for pupils with SEN that is better than that in special schools. Secondly, and related to the first point, the balance of inclusion will be informed by the extent to which special schools are seen to offer something distinctive and helpful beyond the limits of flexibility of a mainstream school. For example, a special school for pupils with profound and multiple learning difficulties might offer:

- a developmentally derived small-steps curriculum;
- assessment of very small steps of progress;
- a distinctive approach to pedagogy such as a 'responsive environment' (Ware 2003); and
- flexibility in organisation such as very small class groups.

Rights and duties

In everyday usage, as indicated by the *Concise Oxford Dictionary* (Allen [ed.] 1990, noun 3), a 'right' is 'a thing one may morally or legally claim; the state of being entitled to a privilege or immunity or authority to act'. There is no indication that the 'claim' may be challenged, or that the 'authority' may be circumscribed or partial. The term 'right' may, therefore, be mistakenly taken to imply a more comprehensive claim than might at first appear.

Similarly, in more philosophical, specifically ethical usage (Mautner [ed.] 1997), a 'right' is seen in three ways:

- as a power;

- in relation to permissibility; and

- in relation to permissibility in conjunction with prohibition of interference.

In the context of a 'right' being regarded as a power, the right is defined as a 'power (an ability, a faculty), belonging to a person, to bring about a change in the moral or legal situation'. One way of doing this is 'by creating an obligation for oneself or for someone else'. To have a right is to be 'in control, morally and legally' (ibid.: 1999). Again, there is no suggestion that the 'right' may be challenged or may be partial. There is an indication, however, that the right can be confirmed by creating an obligation (that is a duty) for someone else.

A duty in general usage, as indicated by the *Concise Oxford Dictionary* (noun 1), is defined as 'a moral or legal obligation'. In this sense, it is something that the person or organisation fulfilling the duty must do.

Four types of legal rights have been suggested (Hohfeld 1923):

1. *Liberty rights* allow you to do something in the sense that you are at liberty to do it. You have a liberty right to use a public facility such as a footpath or a library.

2. *Claim rights* allow you to claim a duty of another person. You have a right not to be assaulted, and another person is placed under a corresponding duty not to assault you.

3. *Legal powers* empower you to do something such as vote in a parliamentary election.

4. *Immunity rights* allow a person to avoid being the subject to the power of another. A disabled person can claim immunity from being drafted into the army.

The concern of this chapter is mainly with 'claim rights', that is a right allowing you to claim a duty of another person. For the right to be meaningful, another person, or persons, is placed under a corresponding duty in the sense that there is something that they must do.

Examples of legal rights relating to special education

The following section considers two examples of legal rights in special education and disability under the Special Educational Needs and Disability Act 2001. These are:

- the right to be educated in the mainstream; and

- certain 'civil' rights for disabled pupils.

The right to be educated in the mainstream

The Education Act 1993, section 160 (later consolidated into the Education Act 1996, section 316), set out for the first time the principle that a child with SEN should, where this was what parents wanted, normally be educated at a mainstream school. There were three conditions: the mainstream provision had to be able to ensure that the child received the educational provision his or her learning difficulty called for; it had to be ensured that others with whom the child with SEN was being educated received efficient education; and resources had to be used efficiently. All three conditions had to be satisfied before mainstream provision was considered appropriate.

The government guidance, *Inclusive Schooling: Children with Special Educational Needs* (Department for Education and Skills 2001a), explains the intention of the Special Educational Needs and Disability Act 2001 (in amending the Education Act 1996, section 316, and in inserting a new section 316A). This, according to *Inclusive Schooling*, is to give a 'strengthened right' to a mainstream education for children with SEN (ibid., para. 4). The fact that the right to a mainstream education is being strengthened suggests (correctly) that the previous 'right' was not comprehensive. The fact that the previous 'right' was circumscribed might alert the reader to the possibility that the new 'right' might also be more limited than might at first appear.

As a result of the Special Educational Needs and Disability Act 2001, the Education Act 1996, section 316(3) was amended to read:

> If a statement is maintained under section 324 for the child, he must be educated in a mainstream school unless that is incompatible with
>
> (a) the wishes of his parent, or
>
> (b) the provision of efficient education for other children.

The use of the word 'must' in the above section of the Act indicates the duty of the LEA and others that complement the right to be educated in the mainstream. If the education of a child with SEN is incompatible with the efficient education of other pupils, mainstream education can only be refused if there are no reasonable steps that can be taken to prevent the incompatibility. But it may not be possible to take steps to prevent a child's inclusion being incompatible with the efficient education of others. This may arise for example:

- when a child's behaviour systematically, persistently and significantly threatens the safety of others;

- when a child's behaviour systematically, persistently and significantly impedes the learning of others;

- where the teacher, even with other support, had to spend a greatly disproportionate amount of time with the child in relation to the rest of the class.

The 'rights' are further effected when one considers a particular school rather than the generic concept of 'mainstream'. A parent may want mainstream provision for their child who has SEN, and may express a preference for a particular mainstream school to be named in their child's statement. In this case, schedule 27 of the Education Act 1996 requires the LEA to name the parents' preferred choice of school in the child's statement unless any of three conditions are not met. These conditions are:

1. the school cannot provide for the needs of the child;

2. the child's inclusion at the school would be incompatible with the efficient education of other pupils; and

3. the child's inclusion at the school would be incompatible with the efficient use of resources.

It will be seen that there is still no comprehensive right of attendance at a mainstream school, but that the rights of the parents of a child with SEN are balanced against the rights of the parents of children who do not have SEN and against other factors.

'Civil' rights for disabled pupils

The guidance, *Inclusive Schooling*, claims that the Special Educational Needs and Disability Act 2001, in amending the Disability Discrimination Act 1995, 'delivers comprehensive enforceable civil rights for disabled pupils and students' (DfES 2001a: 5). For example, schools and local education authorities have new duties to prevent 'discrimination'. They must:

(a) not treat disabled pupils less favourably, without justification, for a reason which relates to their disability;

(b) take reasonable steps to ensure that disabled pupils are not placed at a substantial disadvantage compared to other pupils who are not disabled (but there is no duty to remove or alter physical features or to provide auxiliary aids or services); and

(c) also plan strategically for, and make progress in, improving the physical environment of schools for disabled children, increasing disabled pupils' participation in the curriculum and improving ways in which written information which is provided to pupils who are not disabled is also provided to disabled pupils.

(DfES 2001a: 5)

Just as the legal right to education in the mainstream for pupils with SEN were circumscribed, so it will be seen that the right of disabled pupils not to be considered to be the subject of discrimination is balanced against what is reasonable. If disabled pupils are treated less favourably for a reason that does not relate to their disability, or if it is 'reasonable', it is outside the remit of the Act. Steps taken to ensure that disabled pupils are not placed at a substantial disadvantage compared to other pupils who are not disabled must be 'reasonable'.

The case study below presents a model that helps schools and others to identify, after many interventions have been tried, the level of behavioural, emotional and social difficulty that might lead to a special school placement being considered suitable.

Case study

A model of behaviour support developed in Flintshire LEA (diagram below) indicates the progressive approach to supporting pupils with behavioural, emotional and social difficulties in mainstream and the role of special schools in the structure. These give a picture of the practices at a particular time and, of course, these may change and develop in the future.

The model envisages the level of 'school support' as including certain prerequisites in the mainstream school. These refer to certain policies, agreements, plans and circulars. The school is expected to have a whole-school behaviour policy; an anti-bullying policy; a drug and alcohol policy; and a child protection policy. It should have a home/school agreement. The school should have classroom management plans and individual behaviour plans. Also, it should follow the guidance of Circular 10/99: Social Inclusion: Pupil Support (Department for Education and Employment 1999). This concerns the law and good practice on pupil behaviour and discipline, reducing the risk of disaffection, school attendance and registration, detention, the proper use of exclusion, and the reintegration of excluded pupils.

If the policies, agreements, plans and the following of guidance work effectively, this is expected to lead to a positive outcome. If it does not, then further action is implemented, including the development and implementation of an individual behaviour plan. Should this not have the desired effect, the pupil is considered to be at the 'school support plus', part of the SEN graduated response.

At 'support plus' various agencies are involved and information is exchanged to explore the causes of the behaviour and the possible solutions. This may involve external agencies such as:

- the social services;
- the health service;
- the police;
- the voluntary sector;
- the Youth Offending Team (YOT); and
- the Parents and Family care service.

It may involve LEA support such as:

- the behaviour support service;
- the education welfare officer;

- the educational psychologist;

- special education support services (these include the Learning Support Service and/or the Behaviour Support service);

- the pupil referral unit;

- the education otherwise than at school service (home education by parents supervised by the LEA, and the LEA Home Tuition Service/ Pupil Referral Unit); and

- Youth Access (YA) (a service developed in Wales similar to the Connexions service operationally and with strong vocational and further education links and a real alternative curriculum).

Drawing on such support external and internal to the LEA, the school implements an agreed staged model from the behaviour policy. This involves following the LEA recommendations concerning pupils who do not respond (relating to Circular 10/99). This leads (with internal and external support) to a behaviour-planning meeting to develop a pastoral support programme. The school would produce a pastoral support programme prior to calling in external agencies.

If the school-based pupil support programme is not effective this can result in referral to the behaviour planning group which is a local authority group. This, in turn, may lead to either of three alternatives: school-based education; LEA-based education support; or special education selection.

School-based education may involve: use of the school-based pastoral support programme; reintegration; education based in school with support for a specified limited time; school monitoring; and referral to the discipline committee.

LEA-based support may involve so-called 'engaged pupils' and 'non-engaged pupils'. For 'engaged' pupils, help may be provided by the behaviour support service, the education welfare service and educational psychologists. For non-engaged pupils, provision may involve home tuition, Youth Access or education outside the school.

In the case of special education selection, the pupil is referred for statutory assessment and may receive a statement of SEN. Support may be provided in school, or specialist support may be given. The specialist support might include a combination of learning support, behaviour support, support for the educational psychology service based on the outcome of the assessment and could include the Pastoral Support Plan as well as an Individual Education Plan. Alternatively, the pupil may be educated in a special school either within the LEA or in another LEA.

The model could be supported by a variety of pupil referral unit provision, access via the Behaviour Planning Group and Special Education maintaining links with on-site support provision.

Summary/conclusion

That aspect of inclusion was considered which concerns the balance in mainstream and special schools of pupils with SEN of a severity and complexity that might be thought to justify considering a special school for their education. I suggested that, if educational, social and personal reasons supported the education of pupils in mainstream then this contributed to a moral reason for educating these pupils in mainstream.

In practice, this translates into informing judgements on inclusion by whether or not pupils make better progress academically, socially and personally in a special school or a mainstream school. This, in turn, relates to the flexibility that mainstream schools can achieve in the curriculum, assessment, pedagogy and organisation, and the extent to which special schools provide a distinctive education also in terms of curriculum, assessment, pedagogy and organisation. All this points to a bottom-up approach to inclusion based on what schools and pupils achieve rather than a top-down approach which accepts education in any particular venue as a given good.

The 'inclusion' of pupils with SEN in mainstream schools raises particular issues of balance. On the one hand there are the rights of such pupils and their parents to choose a mainstream education. On the other hand there is the degree to which these rights are, or are not, complemented by the various duties of the LEA and the school as well as consideration of competing rights, such as those relating to other children receiving efficient education. The civil rights of disabled pupils relating to inclusion are similarly balanced against issues such as 'reasonableness', the degree of disadvantage experienced (the interpretation of 'substantial') and other matters.

It is important, given the gloss that can sometimes be put on supposed 'rights', to be aware of when apparent rights are merely one of a number of competing claims that are not always matched by commensurate duties.

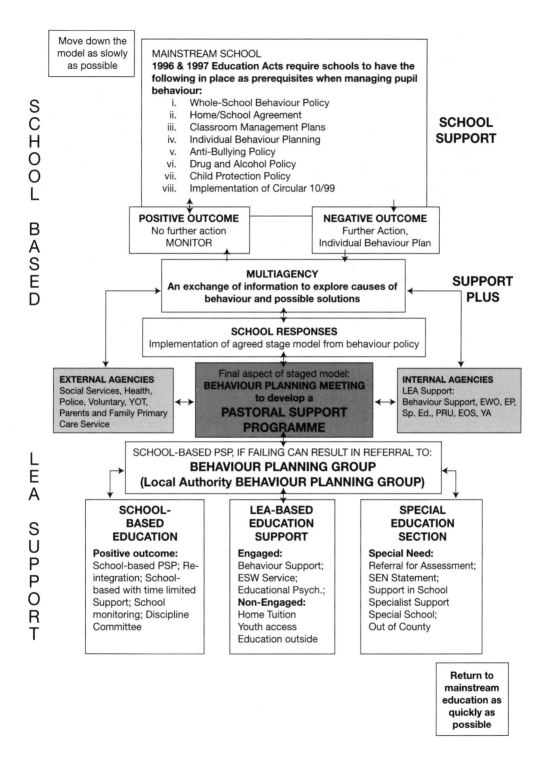

Figure 8.1 A model of behaviour support

Bibliography

Booth, T., Ainscow, M., Black-Hawkins, K., Vaughan, M. and Shaw, L. (2000) *Index for Inclusion: Developing Learning and Participation in Schools*. Bristol: Centre for Studies in Inclusive Education.

Bottomore, T. (1993) *Elites and Society* (2nd edn). London: Routledge.

Brennan, W. K. (1982) *Changing Special Education*. Milton Keynes: Open University Press.

British Psychological Society (1999) *Dyslexia, Literacy and Psychological Assessment: Report by a Working Party of the Division of Educational and Child Psychology of the British Psychological Society*. Leicester: BPS.

Cavanagh, M. (2002) *Against Equality of Opportunity*. Oxford: Oxford University Press.

Dahl, R. A. (1958) 'A critique of the ruling elite model', *American Political Science Review*, **52**.

Dahl, R. A. (1963) *Who Governs: Democracy and Power in an American City*. New Haven, CT: Yale University Press.

Department for Education and Employment (1997) *Excellence for All Children: Meeting Special Educational Needs*. London: DfEE.

Department for Education and Employment (1999a) Circular 10/99: Social Inclusion: Pupil Support. London: DfEE.

Department for Education and Employment (1999b) Circular 11/99: Social Inclusion: The LEA Role in Pupil Support. London: DfEE.

Department for Education and Employment, Scottish Executive, Scotland Office, Cynulliad Cenedlaethol Cymru (2001) *Special Educational Needs and Disability Rights in the Education Act*. London, DfEE *et al*.

Department of Education and Science (1978) *Special Educational Needs: Report of the Committee of Enquiry into the Education of Handicapped Children and Young People 1978: The Warnock Report*. London: DES.

Department for Education and Skills (2001a*) Inclusive Schooling: Children with Special Educational Needs*. London: DfES.

Department for Education and Skills (2001b*) The Special Educational Needs Code of Practice*. London: DfES.

Department for Education and Skills (2001c) *The Distribution of Resources to Support Inclusion.* London: DfES.

Department for Education and Skills (2003a) *Data Collection by Type of Special Educational Needs.* London: DfES.

Department for Education and Skills (2003b) *Report of the Special Schools Working Group.* London: The Stationery Office.

The Disability Rights Commission (2001a) *Code of Practice for Schools.* London: DfES.

The Disability Rights Commission (2001b) *Code of Practice for the Post 16 Sector.* London: DfES.

Farrell, M. (1998) 'New terms for old'. *The SLD Experience*, **21**, Summer, 16–17.

Farrell, M. (2003) *Understanding Special Educational Needs: A Guide for Student Teachers.* London: Routledge.

Farrell, M. (2004) *Special Educational Needs: A Resource for Practitioners.* London: Sage/Paul Chapman.

Favell, J., Realon, R. and Sutton, K. (1996) 'Measuring and increasing the happiness of people with profound mental retardation and physical handicap'. *Behavioural Intervention*, **11** (1), 47–59.

Frederickson, N. and Cline, T. (2002) *Special Educational Needs, Inclusion and Diversity: A Textbook.* Buckingham: Open University Press.

Haywood, A. (1999) *Political Theory: An Introduction* (2nd edn). Basingstoke: Palgrave.

Hendrickson, H. (1997) 'Development of early communication' in Mason, H., McCall, S., Arter, A., McLinden, M. and Stone, J. (eds) *Visual Impairment: Access to Education for Children and Young People.* London: David Fulton.

Hohfeld, W. (1923) *Fundamental Legal Conceptions.* New Haven, CT: Yale University Press.

Hornby, G., Atkinson, M. and Howard, J. (1998) *Controversial Issues in Special Education.* London: David Fulton.

House of Commons (1995) *Meeting Special Educational Needs: Statements of Needs and Provision.* London: Her Majesty's Stationery Office.

Lloyd, L. and Blischak, D. (1992) 'ACC terminology policy and issues update'. *Augmentative and Alternative Communication*, **8** (2), 104–9.

McLinden, M. and McCall, S. (2002) *Learning Through Touch.* London: David Fulton.

Mautner, T. (ed.) (1997) *Penguin Dictionary of Philosophy.* London: Penguin Books.

Mills, C. Wright (1956) *The Power Elite.* New York: Oxford University Press.

Morris, J., Abbott, D. and Ward, L. (2003) 'Disabled children and residential schools: the implications for local education professionals'. *British Journal of Special Education*, **30** (2), 70–5.

Nozick, R. (1974) *Anarchy, State and Utopia.* Oxford: Blackwell.

Office for Standards in Education (2000) *Evaluating Educational Inclusion: Guidance for Inspectors and Schools.* London: Ofsted.

Pavey, B. (2003) 'Citizenship and special educational needs: What are you going to do about teaching them to vote?' *Support for Learning*, **18** (2), 58–65.

Qualifications and Curriculum Authority/Department for Education and Employment (2001) *Planning, Teaching and Assessing the Curriculum for Pupils with Learning Difficulties: General Guidelines*. London: QCA/DfEE.

Rawls, J. (1971) *A Theory of Justice*. Cambridge, MA: Harvard University Press.

Reinders, H. S. (2000) *The Future of the Disabled in a Liberal Society: An Ethical Analysis*. Notre Dame, IA: University of Notre Dame Press.

Special Educational Needs Tribunal (2000) *Annual Report 1999–2000*. London: SEN Tribunal.

Special Educational Needs and Disability Tribunal (2002) *Annual Report 2001–2002*. London: SENDIST.

Thomas, G. (1997) *Exam Performance in Special Schools*. Bristol: CSIE.

Tomlinson, S. (1982) *A Sociology of Special Education*. London: Routledge & Kegan Paul.

Ware, J. (2003) *Creating a Responsive Environment for People with Profound and Multiple Learning Difficulties*. London: David Fulton.

Wedell, K. (2003) 'Points from the SENCO forum: What's in a label?' *British Journal of Special Education*, **30** (2), June, 70–5.

Index

autonomy 80–2

behaviour support model 99
Blackpool Local Education Authority 23–5
Booth, T. 88
Bottomore, T. 65
British Psychological Society 44–5

categories 13, 19–20
    of handicap 12
Cavanagh, M. 32
child
    views of 66–7
civil rights 95–6
cluster funding 48–9
cognition and learning needs 21–2
communication and action needs 22
continua and special educational needs 17
co-operativeness 4, 42–3, 46
criteria 46–7

Dahl, R. A. 52–3
Department for Education and Skills 13,
    16–17, 19, 80, 89, 94
Devon Parent Partnership 71–2
disability 34–8, 66–7
disability interest groups 66–7
Disability Rights Commission 33
discrimination 31–3
diversity 36
duties 6, 92–3

Early Year Action/Plus 20–1

Education Bradford 49–50
Equal opportunities 3, 29–30
    policies 28
Excellence for All Children: Meeting Special
    Educational Needs 89–90

Farrell, M. 7, 90, 91, 92
Favell, J. 80
Flintshire Local Education Authority 96–7
Frederickson, N. and Cline, T. 12

goal-directed need 2, 14–16

Haywood, A. 52, 62
Hohfeld, W. 93

inclusion 6–7, 77–8, 88–92
    future of 9
Index for Inclusion 88–9

labelling 7
Lloyd, L. and Blischak, D. 82
local education authority
    approaches and the Special Educational
        Needs and Disability Tribunal 58–9
    and funding 42

McLinden, M. and McCall, S. 82
mainstream 94–5
Mautner, T. 92
Mills, C. 64
moderation
    of funding decisions 48

moral convictions 79–80

non-normative conditions 18, 44–6
normative conditions 18
Nozick, R. 30–1

Office for Standards in Education (Ofsted) 6

parent 4, 51–2, 59–61
   and lobby groups
   as representatives 68–9
participation 78–9
Pavey, B. 78–9
power 52–5
profound and multiple learning difficulties 5, 77–8, 82–5
Pupil Level Annual School Census (PLASC) 21–2

Qualifications and Curriculum Authority 80

rationality 80–2
Rawls, J. 29
reason 76
Reinders, H. 77–9

representation 64–6
resolving disagreements 55
rights 6, 69, 92–6
   to inclusion 8
   legal 92–6

school clusters 42
school policies 35–6
self-interest 4, 44–6
special educational needs
   definitions of 12–14, 18, 22–3
Special Educational Needs Code of Practice 16, 20–1, 45–6, 53–5, 66–9
Special Educational Needs and Disability Act (2001) 32–5
Special Educational Needs and Disability Tribunal (SENDIST) 4, 51–2, 56–9, 95–6
Special Educational Needs Forum 4–5, 64, 71–2

Tomlinson, S. 18

unconditional need 2, 14–17

Ware, J. 80–1
Warnock Report 13